WOMEN AND CHILDREN LAST

They had no food they had no drink,
At what they done perhaps you'll shrink;
God only knows what it must be,
in an open boat ten days at sea.

Lines from the song 'Fearful Loss of Life at Sea!'
by Charles Fox, 1874

WOMEN AND CHILDREN LAST

THE BURNING OF THE EMIGRANT SHIP *COSPATRICK*

CHARLES R. CLARK

OTAGO

Published by Otago University Press
Level 1, 398 Cumberland Street, Dunedin, New Zealand
Fax: 64 3 479 8385, Email: university.press@stonebow.otago.ac.nz

First published 2006

ISBN 1 877372 14 5

Published with the assistance of the
History Group, Ministry for Culture & Heritage

Front cover image:
'The Only Boat', a lithograph by W.H. Overend.
The Illustrated London News, 1887
Back cover image:
The *Cospatrick*, a watercolour by John Spurling.

Printed through Condor Production Ltd, Hong Kong

CONTENTS

ACKNOWLEDGEMENTS   6

PREFACE   7

1 PROLOGUE   9

2 THE COMPLETE *COSPATRICK*   17

3 SHIPS' BOATS AND THE VICTORIAN SEASCAPE   27

4 A FATAL VOYAGE   53

5 HENRY MCDONALD'S LIFEBOAT   77

6 *COSPATRICK*'S SECOND MATE   87

7 AFTERMATH   103

8 THREE MEN IN A BOAT   121

APPENDICES   131

1 Lifeboat Occupants from the Wreck of the *Cospatrick* 131
2 Verse Inspired by the *Cospatrick* 132
3 Record of *Cospatrick*'s 15 Voyages 138
4 Births and Deaths During *Cospatrick*'s First 14 Voyages 144
5 Register of Accounts of Wages for *Cospatrick*'s
   Deceased Seamen 147
6 Passenger List for the *Cospatrick*'s 15th Voyage 149

NOTES   161

SOURCES OF ILLUSTRATIONS   170

INDEX   171

ACKNOWLEDGEMENTS

The story of the *Cospatrick* is based on material gathered in the United Kingdom, New Zealand and Australia. Librarians and archivists are invariably the most helpful people one could hope to deal with and I am thankful for assistance received at the following institutions: The Bancroft and Local History Library, British Library Newspaper Library, Caird Library (National Maritime Museum), Corporation of London Records Office, Dundee Library, Dundee University Archives, Dunedin Public Library, Family History Centre (Dunedin and London), Guildhall Library, Hocken Library (Dunedin), Llangefni Public Library, Maritime History Archive (Memorial University of Newfoundland), Metropolitan Fire Brigade (London), Montrose Public Library, Merseyside Maritime Museum, National Library of Australia, Otago Settlers' Museum, Public Record Office (now National Archives, London), Singapore Library Archives, Shaftesbury Homes and Arethusa, State Library of Victoria, Tay Valley Historical Society, Turnbull Library (Wellington), University of Otago Library.

The project also benefited from contributions made by various individuals. I am particularly grateful to Bruce E. Collins of Dunedin and Michael Tait of London. I also acknowledge help from the following: Gerard Clark, Dr Geoff Clark, Peter C.R. Collier, Michael Crawford, David Handel Evans, Peglin Faber, Elizabeth Farquhar, Ian J. Farquhar, Dr Russell Frew, Carmela Gallo, Edward Hardman, Trudi Hayes, Mike Hodgkins (HMS *Warrior*), Lorna Hyland, Dr Dafydd Johnston, Kirsten Lawson, Dr John Leader, Kathleen and Stewart Petrie, Maureen Reid, Jan Roberts, Jim Sewell, Dr Paul Sutton, Alison Tait, Dr Margaret Ware and Dr Gail Williams.

The major reference works consulted include: British Sessional Papers (House of Commons), the Captains' Registers; Great Britain Census (1871, 1881, 1891); Great Britain Parliamentary Statutes; Lloyd's List; Lloyd's Register; Register of Births, Deaths and Marriages; and Register of Births, Deaths and Marriages at Sea. Extensive use was made of the Public Record Office file MT 9/99, relating to the Board of Trade Inquiry into the loss of the *Cospatrick*.

PREFACE

Nautical parlance can scarcely be avoided in a book such as this, but I have tried to keep it to a minimum. I have assumed that terms such as bow and stern, port and starboard, and forward and aft are encountered so frequently, even by non-sailors, as to require no explanation. However, others in the text probably do: a jib-boom is the spar projecting forward from the bow of a sailing vessel, and yards are the spars that carry the vessel's square sails. If the vessel happens to be three-masted, then the masts, in sequence from forward to aft, are fore-mast, main-mast and mizzen-mast. The forecastle (pronounced fo'c'sle) and the poop are respectively the raised sections at the forward and after ends of a vessel – on nineteenth century sailing ships these spaces were usually used for accommodation, with the forecastle housing the common seamen, and the poop the vessel's officers and cabin passengers. The word 'deck' occurs frequently and may be ambiguous. It can mean either a single large compartment or a series of compartments situated on the same level (e.g. 'tween deck), or an area to be walked on (e.g. upper deck, main deck); the deck area above the forecastle is known as the forecastle head. A boat's gunwale (pronounced gunnel) is the capping rail above the hull planking, and freeboard is the minimum distance between the top of the gunwale and the surface of the sea. The meaning of other terms should be apparent from the context in which they are used.

Measurements have been expressed in imperial units; distances over water are given in nautical miles; one nautical mile (n.m.) equals 1.151 terrestrial miles or 1.852 kilometres.

I have resisted referring to a ship as 'it'. The term may be acceptable for a modern slab-sided motor vessel, but is scarcely appropriate for the sailing ship of yesterday whose feminine qualities have long been recognised and applauded. Joseph Conrad, the finest of all nautical writers and himself a mariner, believed that a ship should be treated 'with an understanding consideration (for) the mysteries of her feminine nature'. Accordingly, I have followed Conrad and made free use of the feminine pronouns 'her' and 'she'.

CHARLES R. CLARK
Dunedin, October 2005

1. PROLOGUE

A fearful scene it must have been,
On that momentous night;
Oh! may each one of us be spared
Such an appalling sight.
Grim death, alas! was busy there,
In every shape and form;
It was fire did the deadly work
And not the howling storm.

From 'The Ill-fated *Cospatrick*', by J.E. Styles, 5 January 1875

A sea voyage in the nineteenth century was not for the faint-hearted. The hazards were many and accidents commonplace. Each year shipwrecks by the hundred were reported around the coast of the British Isles alone, and each year thousands of British seafarers lost their lives. It was not unusual if a ship failed to arrive at her stated destination – or at any other for that matter. She might founder in the deep oceans, be driven ashore by bad weather or through faulty navigation, or come to grief as a consequence of collision or fire. Britannia may well have ruled the waves, but the seas were hardly docile subjects. Maritime mishaps were so frequent and of such economic and social importance that columns headed 'Shipping Disasters', 'Wrecks and Casualties' or the like appeared daily in British newspapers – and were certainly compelling reading for intending sea travellers.

Of the ways a ship might come to an end, destruction by fire was perhaps the most feared. Few sights were more sobering than that of a burning vessel at sea – abandoned most likely, masts fallen, ironwork glowing red-hot, and leaving such a smoke trail to leeward that her plight was signalled long before the hull became visible – and all this while she was surrounded by the very medium necessary to extinguish the blaze. Wooden sailing vessels were particularly vulnerable; inherently flammable, they lacked the interior partitions (bulkheads) that increased the chance for an outbreak to be contained. Nineteenth-century shipboard fire-fighting equipment was rudimentary, and it was not until the very end of the era that fire extinguishers and breathing apparatus came into general use. Without breathing apparatus, it was next to impossible to fight a fire below decks. Fire-pumps were manually operated for the most part, and were relatively ineffective; back-breaking work at the pump handles might be rewarded with little by way of water-flow at the business end of the hose. Perhaps indicative of a fatalistic attitude among seafarers, fire-drills – like boat-drills – rarely figured in a ship's routine and were often neglected entirely.

The period saw a number of catastrophic shipboard fires, but that involving the New Zealand-bound emigrant ship *Cospatrick* was certainly the most destructive. The elderly *Cospatrick* sank after catching fire in the South Atlantic on 18 November 1874, and of her complement of nearly 500 people – men, women and children – only three survived. Widely regarded as the most horrific disaster to befall a British merchant vessel during the Victorian era, the episode had all the ingredients to justify a notorious reputation: a desperate battle to quench the fire was followed by chaos as the inadequacies of the ship's boats became apparent, a huge death toll as the vessel was being abandoned, and acts of cannibalism in the one lifeboat to remain afloat.

Coincidentally, the situation that developed in *Cospatrick*'s lifeboat was foreshadowed by two other incidents in 1874 – also involving British vessels burnt at sea. The first occurred when the collier *Arracan*, out of Shields and bound for Bombay, was abandoned in flames on 14 February after her cargo of coal ignited (spontaneous combustion of coal cargoes was a frequent cause of nineteenth-century ship losses). With no passengers to complicate matters, the crew left the ship in three boats. One was soon picked up by a passing vessel, while another made a landfall in Cochin China (now Vietnam). The third, a pinnace under the command of Dundee-born second mate David Webster and containing three seamen and a ship's boy named Horner, drifted on the Indian Ocean for four and a half weeks. The boat had been well provisioned before leaving the collier and the supplies, carefully eked out, lasted 19 days. But two days after the last morsel had been consumed, the seamen cast lots and decided that Horner would be sacrificed for food. Just how the lottery was carried out is not known, but it was almost certainly rigged; in similar situations it was often arranged for the weakest or least popular person in the boat to draw the short straw. Webster had been asleep during proceedings but awoke in time to save the boy's life. Having had the presence of mind to arm himself before leaving the *Arracan*, he defended Horner and threatened to shoot the first man to lay a hand on him. This averted the immediate danger but tension remained extreme. During the next three days several attempts were made on Webster's life, and a sailor twice tried to sink the boat. The same man also endeavoured to kill Horner, an act for which he would have been shot had Webster's gun not misfired. Shortly after this incident, a fortunate encounter with a stray seabird relieved much of the pressure. The bird was shot by Webster and avidly consumed – 'flesh, feathers, bones and all'.[1] An uneasy truce then settled over the boat, with the occupants managing to subsist on 'sea blubber' and barnacles growing on its underside. Webster and Horner kept watch by turn, neither daring to sleep unless the other was awake. When a seaman named Layford reached the limit of endurance he asked to be killed, whereupon one of his mates struck him repeatedly about the head with an iron belaying pin. Both men had earlier drunk large amounts of seawater, a substance not particularly conducive to sensible decision-making. Layford, however, survived the onslaught and the blood that flowed from his wounds – copious amounts according to one report – was caught in a tin and eagerly shared between the two. Subsequently victim and attacker 'fought and bit one another', and then 'shook hands and laughed and kissed one another like madmen.'[2] After 31 days at sea the pinnace fell in with the steamer *City of Manchester* and the five people in her, 'unable to stand on their feet, eyes starting from their sockets and perfect skeletons,' were taken on board.[3] Webster was later awarded the Albert Medal for saving the life of everyone in the boat.

The second incident ended far less satisfactorily. The five seamen from the vessel *Euxine*, who 'from necessity' killed and partially consumed a fellow sailor, were prosecuted to the fullest extent of the law. This case appears to have been the first in which British shipwreck survivors were charged with murder after doing away with a shipmate to secure their own survival. *Euxine*'s crew took to the boats on 8 August 1874 and 20-year-old Able Seaman Francis Gioffus (or Gioffous; in contemporary reports he is often referred to as Shufus) was sacrificed 23 days later. The cause of his death, recorded in the Register of Accounts of Wages and Effects of Deceased Seamen as 'killed by boat's crew for food', represents one of this register's more unusual entries.[4]

The *Euxine* and *Arracan* incidents had much in common. *Euxine*, also out of Shields with coal for the East, suffered storm damage, lost one man overboard, and developed a severe list after experiencing a cargo shift during a South Atlantic gale on 1 August 1874. For three days and nights the crew worked frenziedly to right the vessel. Much of the cargo was jettisoned and the list had just been corrected when it became apparent that the remaining coal was on fire. *Euxine*'s captain, Peter Murdoch, ordered the hatches battened down and set a course for the island of St Helena. Despite the best efforts of the sailors, the fire gained and the vessel was abandoned in flames, having fallen short of this target by 850 miles. Murdoch, a man of energy and foresight, made sure that the three boats that left the collier were sound, properly provisioned and well equipped.[5] His own, together with that of the chief mate, landed safely on St Helena 10 days after *Euxine*'s abandonment, but the third ran into difficulties.

This was a boat commanded by James Archer, *Euxine*'s 24-year-old second mate. Like David Webster of the *Arracan*, Archer hailed from Dundee. His boat was 30 feet long and equipped with 10 air-cases for buoyancy. A canvas strip raised around the sides to form bulwarks increased its seaworthiness. Thanks to Murdoch, it had been provided with drinking water in two small casks, two boxes of ship's biscuit, a ham, a cheese, about 20 tins of meat and some tinned soup. Four pounds of tobacco included among the supplies did much to uplift the sailors' spirits. The boat was equipped with navigational instruments, and was properly rigged and carried a good set of sails. In addition to Archer, it contained the ship's boatswain, Peter Jackson (or de Jager), Ordinary Seaman George Reynolds, and five able seamen: Victor Sandström, Alexander Vermeulen, August Müller, Manus Schutt and Gioffus.

Archer's boat lost contact with the others during the first night at sea.

Its crew spent 12 days sailing toward St Helena, then two more casting about in a fruitless search for the island. Eventually figuring the boat was too far to the west, Archer decided to try and reach the Brazilian coast 1800 miles away – it was a not a wise decision. He had originally set the food allowance as two biscuits and one pint of water per man per day, together with a small piece of cheese and ham. With provisions running short, he cut this ration in two. One biscuit, half a pint of water, and a portion of tinned meat was little enough as daily sustenance for a man, but the weather continued fine and the boat made good progress. Two or three flying fish were caught, and although some rain fell it was only light drizzle 'which served only to make them uncomfortable.'[6] But as the food and freshwater supplies dwindled, so too did morale. Jackson, the boatswain, grew increasingly despondent and on two occasions had to be prevented from knocking a hole in the boat 'to put an end to the misery of all'.[7]

On 27 August it came on to blow. At 11 p.m. Jackson fell asleep while steering and released his hold on the tiller. The boat swung broadside to the waves and capsized when hit by a heavy sea. All eight men were flung into the water.

Bright moonlight fell on a desolate scene. George Reynolds had wrapped himself in a blanket and drowned while trapped in its folds. Schutt, a good swimmer, was seized by Jackson while trying to rescue Vermeulen. Unable to save both, he kicked free of Jackson's grasp and succeeded in bringing Vermeulen to the uncertain security of the upside-down boat. For a time Jackson held onto a floating biscuit box, but lost his grip and also drowned. Archer, Gioffus, Sandström, and Müller recovered sufficiently to make their way to the capsized craft and, together with Schutt and Vermeulen, clung to its upturned keel until dawn. Greatly weakened by their ordeal, the men succeeded in righting the boat only on the fourth attempt. Although full of water, it floated gunwale-deep owing to its air-cases.

As the boat was being baled out it was discovered that the water casks had filled with salt water, and that of the food supplies only one tin of kidney soup remained. The compass and sextant were missing, along with other vital equipment – the masts had been swept away as had nearly all the rigging. But a jury rig consisting of bottom boards and half an oar was improvised, and the gunwale canvas stripped off and put to use as a makeshift sail. Archer, navigating by the sun, continued to sail the boat toward the Brazilian coast, but at vastly reduced speed.

Tormented by increasing thirst, the survivors were soon reduced to drinking seawater. According to Archer, Müller drank more than the others and by the morning of 31 August was delirious. He then 'declared that he offered his body to serve as food for the others and entreated the others to kill and devour him'.[8] This generous offer was declined but events took an equally dramatic course. Müller may not have been quite as deranged as Archer's description suggests. His own testimony records that

> ... the hunger and thirst were fearful. I tried to relieve myself by drinking saltwater but the pangs of thirst always came back. We looked round and round ever so many times to discover a sail or something. We felt all exhausted. No sleep could be had as we constantly got wet from water coming in and our stomachs never ceased gnawing ... On the morning of the fourth day after capsizing I heard Bill [Manus] Schutt say that we should draw lots [to decide] who should perish to keep the others alive. This was done after some time. The things for a lottery were made of sticks cut from boards. We agreed that it should be decided after three drawings ...[9]

Archer readily agreed to the lottery, possibly because dissent in such circumstances might well have proved fatal to himself. His own account records that he held the sticks for the first draw, whereas Müller said that Sandström held them. But except for this minor discrepancy the depositions of the five who survived are in agreement.[10] On the first and second draws, Gioffus was the one who drew the shortest stick. As the third draw was about to be performed, he baulked. Müller's statement continues:

> When it was time for the Italian to pull out a piece of wood he hesitated and said he would not draw. Upon this, as the Italian had previously consented and agreed to take part in the lottery, Sandström said that he would draw for Shufus. On comparing the pieces of wood together it was found that the one which Sandström had taken out for Shufus was the shortest.

Gioffus's fate was thus sealed, even though the mathematical chance of the same individual being selected from six on three successive occasions is just one in 216 – not impossibly long odds, but certainly long enough to suggest that the lottery was contrived. The Italian appears to have been the odd man out in the boat: unpopular and apparently having little English apart from 'yes' and 'no', he may well have been unaware of what had been arranged by the others. He was given an hour's grace, which he spent in prayer. Apparently passive, he was then bound by Müller, whose first attempt at execution with a dull sheath knife was not surprisingly botched: 'I held the knife and gave him a cut across the nape of the neck, but as the knife was not sharp enough to penetrate through I had to put it around his throat. Sandström caught the blood in a pannikin.' Müller cut out Gioffus's heart and liver, which were sliced into small pieces and mixed with blood and seawater before being consumed. All five men participated in the feast, with some gnawing on the arms. Müller then 'cleaned the body and cut it in pieces by the joints'; the head and hands were thrown overboard and the trunk and limbs stowed in one of the boat's air-cases, which had been cut open for the purpose. Almost immediately after this gruesome restocking of the food supplies, the Dutch ship *Java Packet* hove into view. As soon as the survivors realised they were certain to be picked up, most of the evidence of cannibalism was disposed of over the side, but the boat's blood-spattered interior (and a piece of liver which had been overlooked) left their rescuers in little doubt as to what had happened. The *Java Packet* carried them to Batavia (now Jakarta), where they arrived on 2 November.

The men freely admitted to killing Gioffus on the grounds of necessity, and made formal statements to this effect before William T. Fraser, Her Britannic Majesty's Acting Consul in Batavia. They were then sent to Singapore, taken into custody, and charged with murder by the colonial authorities. Various appearances at the Singapore Police Court followed, before it was decided that the Singapore judiciary lacked the authority to try the prisoners and that they should face trial in England. An important witness at the preliminary hearings was Singapore's Shipping Attendant, Henry Ellis, who had received the depositions of the accused and forwarded them to the Board of Trade in London. Ellis, formerly a ship's captain, had once spent two days in an open boat without fresh water. This reduced him to 'such a state as he hoped never to be in again' and to drinking seawater. Openly sympathetic to the survivors, Ellis told the court that he was aware 'of cases of drawing lots among shipwrecked persons as to whom should die for the rest … and had never heard of men punished for so doing.'[11] Presumably he had himself been driven to contemplate acts similar to those carried out in *Euxine's* boat. But in other quarters the conduct of the five survivors was viewed less compassionately.

News of the *Euxine* incident reached Britain toward the end of December.[12] Men who in all probability had never missed a meal in their lives pondered the case, and the fate of the boat crew was debated in high places. Thomas Gray, an assistant secretary of the Board of Trade with responsibility for the Marine Department, was one who thought it unlikely any jury would find against the men. Schutt had been persuaded to turn Queen's evidence, but much rested on Ellis's testimony and he was hostile to the prosecution. As acquittal might signal approval for all acts of murder carried out on the grounds of necessity, Gray pointed out the dangers of such a precedent, for 'if a court of law were to stamp this custom with clear authority it might be made a pretext for getting rid of troublesome people.'[13] This concern certainly contributed to charges against Müller, Archer, Vermuelen and Sandström being dropped on 22 July 1875, just 13 days after the men had arrived in Britain following their illegally enforced return from Singapore on the steamship *Nestor*.[14] Public reaction to the *Euxine* incident was generally low-key, but an extensive article in the *Montrose Standard* of 1 January 1875 condemned the 'wretched creatures' who 'had only been three days without water when they commenced the suicidal folly of drinking from the sea'. Apparently unaware of Archer's Dundee connections, the writer was scathing of his conduct, comparing it unfavourably with that of 'a young Scotchman' (*Arracan's* David Webster) who had been placed in the same dilemma. On the same day as this article was being read on the streets of Montrose, Henry McDonald, another 'young Scotchman' and a resident of the town, had arrived in London to face similar scrutiny regarding his behaviour in a lifeboat from the *Cospatrick*.

2. THE COMPLETE COSPATRICK

*She had conveyed thousands of soldiers –
her deck planks were worn to hollows by their boots.*

Edward Cotter, referring to the *Cospatrick*[1]

The *Cospatrick* was a two-decked, three-masted sailing ship of 1199 tons, constructed of teak at Moulmein, Burma, and completed on 18 August 1856. Built in what was known as the Blackwall Frigate style, she was heavily timbered, bluff-bowed, and beamy. Many elements of her design harked back to an earlier generation of merchant shipping, and her square stern, quarter galleries and stern windows were unfashionable even at the time she was launched. *Cospatrick* was ship-rigged (carrying square sails on all masts) and her dimensions were 191 by 34 by 23½ feet (length, breadth, depth of hold). The first record of her movements in Lloyd's List indicates that, with G. Hodge as captain, she arrived at London from Moulmein *via* St Helena on 8 August 1857. In the same year she was rated A1 at Lloyd's for 15 years – a classification which was extended for a further 14 years in 1869. She was registered in London, with official number 20,400 and signal code MWVT. In a career spanning 18 years and encompassing 14 round-trip voyages out of her home port, the *Cospatrick* was commanded by just three men: Charles Scott (1858–62), James Aberdour Elmslie (1862–67) and James's younger brother, Alexander (1867–74). At least 88 passenger deaths and 23 births occurred on the vessel before her uncompleted 15th voyage in 1874. Causes of death among those who took passage on the *Cospatrick* ranged from secondary syphilis and drowning after falling overboard, to measles and dysentery. As with most other vessels of the time, fatalities among the very young were usually due to gastro-intestinal complaints.

Cospatrick's first owner was Duncan Dunbar, a London-based shipowner and a significant figure in British shipping circles. In 1825 Dunbar inherited a few coastal vessels from his Scottish father, and from this modest beginning went on to create the largest privately owned fleet in the world. By 1855, a time when a ship of 1000 tons was still considered a large vessel, his fleet totalled 40,000 tons.[2] In later life he was chairman of both the General Ship-owners Association and the London Chartered Bank of Australia, and was deputy chairman of the East and West India Dock Company. It was said that his prosperity was due to the fondness of Australian palates for Taylor, Walker & Co. beer, which Dunbar vessels transported to the colony in huge volumes – his shipping operations were centred on the Dunbar Wharf at Limehouse, conveniently close to Taylor, Walker & Co.'s Barley Mow Brewery.[3]

Despite his business acumen, Dunbar is remembered in maritime circles for an association with 'unlucky' ships; this reputation is based largely on the wreck of the clipper ship *Dunbar* at the Sydney Heads in 1857, on the sinking of the Dunbar-built *Northfleet* following a collision off Dungeness in 1873, and, of course, on the 1874 burning of the *Cospatrick*. The combined death toll in these three disasters amounted to nearly 900 passengers and crew, with fewer than 90 persons surviving. Dunbar's apparent link with misfortune is emphasised by other losses, such as that of the *Duncan Dunbar* on the coast of Brazil in 1865, and the Dunbar-owned *Blervie Castle*, which sank in the English Channel with the loss of all on board in 1859.

The red lion rampant adorning the company house flag reflected Dunbar's pride in his Scottish heritage and a fervent nationalism. Many of his vessels were named after British military victories, although others were given family names; the *Cospatrick* was named for his eleventh-century ancestor Cospatrick, Earl of Northumberland. As a new ship with roomy and well-ventilated 'tween decks she was regarded as ideal for troopship duty, and, under charter to Her Majesty's Council of India, fulfilled this role on four successive voyages to the subcontinent following the Indian Mutiny of 1857. When Dunbar died suddenly at his Kensington home on 6 March 1862 at 58 years of age, the *Cospatrick* was engaged on hospital-ship duties; homeward bound on the fourth of these voyages, she was returning from Bombay with more than 200 rank-and-file invalids and

Duncan Dunbar,
1804–62.

insane soldiers. Dunbar's death brought an abrupt end to his shipping empire. He had accumulated a huge personal fortune but left no heir capable of taking over the company. His ships were sold, with the chief beneficiaries from the estate (reported by *The Times* to be worth £1.5 million)[4] being his sisters, Margaret Masson and Phoebe Dunbar, and the children of his deceased sister Isobel Abbott. *Cospatrick* then passed into the ownership of another London-based shipping firm, Smith, Fleming & Co.

Cospatrick continued to be employed as a troopship to India, but some months after the change of ownership was chartered by the Indian Government to assist in transporting out and laying the 1864 Persian Gulf Submarine Telegraph Cable. She was temporarily fitted out for cable-laying at Woolwich, and on 27 November 1863 sailed from Gravesend for Bombay carrying 101.5 n.m. of deep-sea cable, 23 n.m. of shore ends and 12 n.m. of double armoured shore ends. Deep-sea cable-laying techniques were comparatively primitive at this time; failure rates were high and the similar Red Sea and India Telegraph Cable of 1859 had proved a fiasco. However, the *Cospatrick* and four other sailing vessels (*Marion Moore*, *Kirkham*, *Tweed*, and *Assaye*) successfully laid a total of 1450 miles of submarine cable (of weight 5028 tons) in four bights across the stretches of water now known as The Gulf and the Northern Arabian Sea. Extending from Fāo (Iraq) in the west to Karachi in the east, the cable touched at Bushire (now Būshehr, Iran), Cape Mussendom (now Musandam, Oman) and Gwadar (Pakistan). *Cospatrick* and *Assaye* laid the final section between Gwadar and Karachi while under tow from the Indian Government steamer *Amberwitch*.[5] The 1864 Persian Gulf cable was of particular significance to Far Eastern commerce as it connected to existing landlines and, for the first time, allowed telegraphic communication between India and Europe.

The *Cospatrick* made two voyages to Australia: the first was to Sydney with passengers and general cargo in 1867, and the second to Melbourne with emigrants in 1870–71. At the end of the Melbourne passage 443 men, women and children were landed at Port Phillip on or about 13 March 1871. Even greater numbers were carried on other occasions. At least 570 were on board during the vessel's 1858 passage to Calcutta, and of these no fewer than 532 were either soldiers or their dependants. *Cospatrick*'s career as a troopship came to an end on 27 November 1868, when reinforcements for various cavalry and artillery units (totalling 362 persons inclusive of accompanying family members) were landed at Karachi following a 116-day passage from Gravesend. The opening of Suez Canal in 1869 signalled the end of trooping to India via the Cape of Good Hope. Sailing vessels such as the *Cospatrick* were not adapted to the more direct canal route, nor could they match the efficiencies of the steam-powered Royal Navy troopships that were. Like other owners engaged in the trade, Smith, Fleming & Co. sought alternative employment for their vessel.

Early in 1873 *Cospatrick* came to the notice of Shaw, Savill & Co., and she was purchased from Smith, Fleming for £11,000 on 7 March. Interest in the vessel was divided between Walter Savill, James Temple, James Adamson, Thomas Ronaldson (12/64ths each), and John Parker (16/64ths). Shaw, Savill & Co. (later to become Shaw, Savill

Walter Savill, 1836–1911; an 1870 oil portrait by C. Van Lil.

& Albion through amalgamation with the Albion Line in 1882) had been formed in 1858 by the partnership of Walter Savill (b. 1836) and Robert Shaw (b. 1823). The fledgling London-based company survived Shaw's premature death from a heart attack in 1864 and under Savill's vigorous management soon became the most important shipping firm engaged in the New Zealand trade. James Temple was brought in as a partner following Shaw's death. Savill was one of five brothers who variously established themselves in the City of London during the middle of the nineteenth century. In a play on the Savill name, and reflecting individual characteristics of three of the brothers, Alfred, the eldest, became known in business circles as 'Save All', Walter as 'Grab All', and the youngest, Martin, well established in society through his marriage to the Lord Mayor's daughter, as 'Spend All'. Walter Savill was the archetypal Victorian businessman – in later life, according to his biographer, frugal to the point of refusing monetary allowances to his sons, and known to avoid them on the street for fear they would ask for money.[6] In 1873 his company faced intense competition from the newly formed New Zealand Shipping Company, and was hastily buying ships to take advantage of New Zealand's rapidly accelerating development. The country had entered a period of calm after the land wars, a rail network was being established and wages were high for those prepared to work hard. A generous government-sponsored emigration scheme, promoted through extensive advertising in Britain's provincial newspapers (and backed by letters from migrants who found the country to their liking), encouraged British workers to take the first steps on what they believed would be a 15,000 mile journey to prosperity. Savill had tied his fortune to that of New Zealand and was anticipating a large increase in trade. His company acquired 11 sailing ships in 1873 (one was the teak-built *Edwin Fox*, which survives as a hulk in Picton, New Zealand), and vessels either owned or chartered by Shaw Savill made 67 sailings to the colony during the year.[7] The *Cospatrick* was despatched to Otago with 45 passengers and a general cargo on 21 March, just two weeks after her purchase had been finalised. Alexander Elmslie, a 39-year-old Scot who had commanded the vessel since 1867, continued as captain despite the change in ownership.

Her outward passage of 108 days between Gravesend and Port Chalmers was, according to a report compiled from her log, 'characterised by anything but favourable weather, but notwithstanding the heavy weather encountered, the vessel – a staunch and strong one – seems to have battled it out well, and is brought into port in good order, reflecting on master and officers.' This in spite of 'a terrific gale during which she lost several new sails, and while scudding under the lower main topsail and foresail [was struck by a] heavy sea – knocking in her dead lights, washing tons of water into the cuddy, destroying all the captain's clothing, books and charts, and damaging stores.'[8] Of course, many other New Zealand-bound sailing vessels received similar storm damage – or worse – while running their easting down in the tempestuous Southern Ocean.

Cospatrick sailed in ballast from Port Chalmers for Newcastle, Australia on 26 August 1873. Eleven seamen had deserted during her stay – not a sign of a happy ship – while another was left behind in hospital. At Newcastle the vessel loaded coal for Calcutta and, on reaching that port and discharging her cargo, departed for Cayenne, French Guiana by

The *Cospatrick* photographed at Port Chalmers in 1873. (Photo D.A. DeMaus)

way of St Helena on 23 December. It was this segment of the voyage that prompted one of the survivors of her sinking to later describe the *Cospatrick* as 'something of a blackbirder' – an observation suggesting she was carrying slaves.[9] *Cospatrick*'s passengers were in fact coolies (from the Hindi *kuli*, or labourer) and, of the 481 embarked at Calcutta, 22 died during the 92-day passage to Cayenne. Eighteen of the deaths occurred before the vessel called at St Helena on 28 February 1874.[10] Dissatisfaction and dissent marked this section of the voyage and the names of several seamen were entered in the log for refusing to obey legitimate orders. On one occasion Able Seaman Stephen Fearon deliberately placed the vessel in danger when he walked from the wheel while the *Cospatrick* was running before a fresh breeze.[11] At St Helena the island's emigration officer reported *Cospatrick*'s coolies to be 'clean and in good order, happy and contented with food and treatment', but this could hardly have been the case.[12] Ship's biscuit was being bartered

Charles Henry McDonald,
1845–85. *(The Graphic, 1875).*

for sexual favours and shortly after the vessel's brief visit, Elmslie found it necessary to upbraid his crew for 'having communion with some of the female emigrants and likewise beating and ill-treating some of the male emigrants.'[13] Deliberate neglect and abuse of passengers was commonplace in the West Indian coolie trade, with disease introduced at the port of embarkation responsible for high mortality rates. The *Forfarshire*, also a Shaw Savill vessel, recorded 52 deaths (30 of which occurred during a single five-day period) while on a similar voyage in 1875.[14] In the 25 months from 12 January 1872 to 28 February 1874, 27,086 Indian coolies were transported to the West Indies in 59 British ships. Of this number 1162 died *en route* – an average of 20 deaths per voyage; this in spite of all ships being required to carry a European surgeon. Worst of all, the *Golden Fleece* had 68 deaths among 524 coolies in 1873.[15]

After *Cospatrick*'s coolies were disembarked at Cayenne, the vessel proceeded to Demerara, British Guiana, to load sugar and rum for London. Henry McDonald, recently paid off from the barque *Heath Park*, was given the opportunity to join the ship when First Mate Walter Walpole and 13 sailors were discharged 'by mutual consent'.[16] *Cospatrick*'s second mate, Charles Lewis Romaine, was promoted to fill the vacancy created by Walpole's departure, and on 12 May 1874 McDonald was taken on as Romaine's replacement.[17] Tall and lean, with black hair and a swarthy complexion, McDonald at 29 years of age was a competent seaman. Considerably experienced in the Baltic and West Indian shipping trades, he had also voyaged to New Zealand and Canada.

The *Cospatrick* arrived back in London at the end of June 1874. Damage to her keel (caused by touching on a reef during the voyage) was repaired 'in a good substantial manner' in Green's dry-dock in July.[18] When surveyed in August, much of the vessel's standing and running rigging had been renewed, and Greens had replaced her jib-boom and all three topsail yards. Shaw Savill had secured a charter with the New Zealand Government for her to carry emigrants to Auckland in addition to a general cargo that was to be loaded at the East India Docks. While in London, *Cospatrick* was for a time moored alongside Shaw Savill's 746-ton iron barque *Langstone*. In a fateful decision, Henry McDonald declined the offer of the second mate's position in her, preferring to stay where he was.

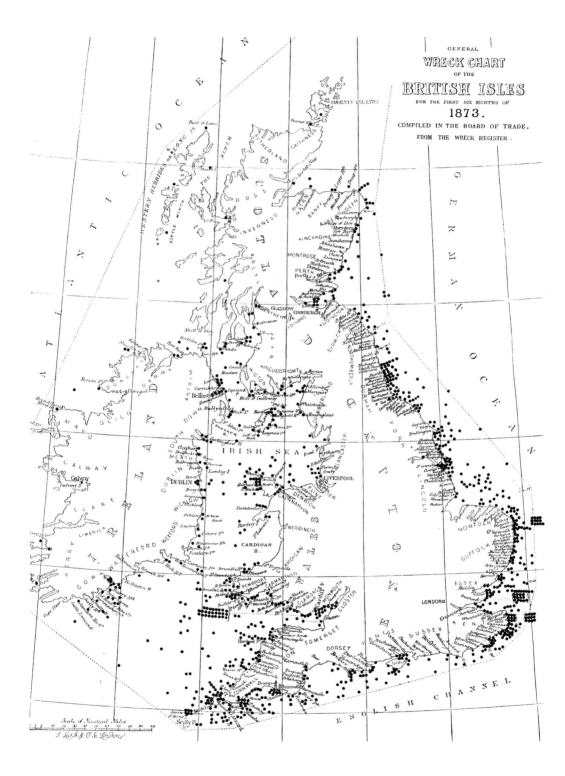

Locations of the approximately 800 ship casualties that occurred on and around the coast of Great Britain during the first six months of 1873. (*The Graphic*)

3. Ships' Boats and the Victorian Seascape

… there is, patently and confessedly, only boat accommodation for one half of the 600 people we have on board … having once seen the terrible death struggle for places in boats from a sinking ship, I do not wish to see it again – especially so women and children fighting for their lives with men.

Excerpt from a letter to *The Times* of 21 September 1872
from a passenger on board the steamship *Atrato*

'**W**omen and children first!*'* was a cry that epitomised a well-known Victorian convention. If a disaster occurred at sea, it was generally held that the rescue of women and children should take priority over the rescue of men. Rightly or wrongly, the ideal became associated with a powerful image – one of a storm-tossed sea and a vessel in distress, of women and children being passed into a lifeboat by the caring hands of the crew, and of men-folk stoically standing by as the ship sank beneath them; a melodramatic image, but one with great appeal to the nineteenth-century British public. Hidden in the picture, of course, is the uncomfortable suggestion that not everything was done to ensure ships of the time were provided with the means to save life. If one boat could leave the vessel safely, why was it not followed by a second – and a third? Why were there not sufficient boats to accommodate everyone on board?

The frequency of shipwreck during the mid to latter part of the nineteenth century was nothing less than remarkable. In addition to the huge numbers of British ships lost each year on and around the coast of Great Britain, dozens more were wrecked elsewhere – or left port never to be seen or heard of again. The magnitude of the problem may be judged from the fact that British merchant ship casualties and attendant loss of life for the nine-year period 1875 to 1883 was officially estimated as 10,318 ships, 21,224 seamen and 3392 passengers.[1] Misadventure at sea was not only a major cause of accidental death, but the loss of a passenger or emigrant vessel (this was a time when the two were not always distinguishable) could provide a civil catastrophe on the largest scale. Many of these barely remembered incidents involved a loss of life so great – often the dead numbered in the hundreds – that each became briefly notorious, the focus of public attention only until displaced by the next. In this respect they were similar to passenger aircraft disasters of a much later era.

Some ships were lost with all hands, most notably the *City of Glasgow*, which disappeared along with 373 passengers and crew while on a voyage from Liverpool to New York in 1854, and the *Sir John Lawrence* – sunk in the Bay of Bengal with a death toll of at least 776 in 1887. But there were many other instances where some fraction of those on board a sinking passenger vessel lived through the catastrophe while hundreds died around them. On these occasions women and children were rarely found among the survivors, no matter how frequently they were represented in the passenger lists; survival rates for women and children as a group were nearly always dramatically lower than for adult male passengers and crew members. This statistical bias occurred irrespective of whether the ship had been driven ashore, or had sunk following storm, collision or fire at sea. Contrary to popular belief, the rescue of women and children was rarely a priority once difficulties were experienced as a vessel was being abandoned – more often than not they came last in the race for survival.

Between 1850 and 1900 there were seven 'survivable' wrecks of British passenger ships in which the death toll on each occasion exceeded 290 souls. The vessels involved were the *Tayleur* (1854), *Royal Charter* (1859), *Northfleet* (1873), *Atlantic* (1873), *Cospatrick* (1874), *Kapunda* (1887), and *Utopia* (1891).[2] A total of 2960 people lost their lives in these major incidents, while about 1160 survived. Of those who lived, 209 (from a total of 510) were sailors, while 929 (from a total of 2370) were adult male passengers – overall a survival rate of about 40 per cent for both groups. Of the 1260 women and children who had taken passage on the seven ships, fewer than 20 survived – overall a survival rate of less than 2 per cent. The figures for married men travelling with their families are less certain, but suggest a survival rate similar to that of the women and children. The survival patterns in the individual incidents are given in the table on page 31.

The emigrant ship *Utopia* (Anchor Line) sinks in Gibraltar Harbour after a collision with the battleship HMS *Anson* in 1891. *Utopia* had only 160 lifejackets for her 875 passengers and crew, despite 1890 maritime legislation requiring one for each person. (The *Illustrated London News*, 1891)

The fact that only three of *Cospatrick*'s complement of 479 lived through her burning places this incident as the 'least survivable' of the seven. The sinking of the Australia-bound emigrant vessel *Kapunda* after a mid-Atlantic collision ranks as the second 'least survivable'; just 16 of *Kapunda*'s complement of 314 survived. If the number of lives lost is taken as the criterion, then the disasters which befell the *Atlantic* (546 dead) and the *Utopia* (562 dead) are certainly the worst: of the 283 women and children on *Atlantic* only one child was saved, although more than 400 adult male passengers and crew members survived. All 253 women and children travelling on the *Cospatrick* at the time of her destruction lost their lives.

Six of the seven ships came to grief at night (the exception was the *Tayleur*). Darkness carried its own hazards and invariably made a bad situation worse. Below deck, spaces were poorly lit and above decks little better. A lack of lighting added to the sense of confusion and panic as a vessel was being abandoned. When the grotesquely named *Utopia* sank after a collision in Gibraltar Harbour one evening at dusk, the death toll would have been higher than 562 had the scene not been illuminated by the searchlights of the assembled British Mediterranean Fleet. This was probably the first occasion when electric lighting was used during a maritime rescue, but only about 10 of the 152 women and children on *Utopia* survived. All 60 single women on the *Kapunda* died after their ship collided with the barque *Ada Melmore* at 3.25 a.m. on 20 January 1887. Following regulations prevalent on emigrant ships of the time, the women had been locked into their compartment at nightfall – a measure that preserved their chastity but not their lives. 'The shrieks of the women pierced the air for a considerable distance' and their compartment door was still locked when the vessel rolled onto her beam-ends and slipped beneath the surface. Contemporary accounts did not dwell on the desperate struggles of the females trapped in *Kapunda*'s after compartment. After all, according to *The Times*, 'most if not all of them would have swooned by the crushing and the intense excitement.'[3]

The myth of 'Women and children first' had its origins in the sinking of Her Majesty's Ship *Birkenhead* off the coast of Southern Africa in the early hours of 26 February 1852. The vessel had arrived at Simon's Bay near Cape Town on the twenty-fourth, with drafts from various regiments (2nd (Queen's) Foot, 6th Regt., 12th Lancers, 12th Regt., 43rd Light Infantry, 50th Rifles, 73rd Regt., 74th Regt., and 91st Foot), destined as reinforcements for forces engaged in the 8th Kaffir War. Accompanying the troops were 25 women and 31 children, most of whom were landed shortly after arrival. During the voyage out from Cork, four women had died and there had been three births, but *Birkenhead*, which possessed a large and well-disciplined Royal Navy crew, was first and foremost a troopship rather than a passenger vessel in the usual sense. At 6 p.m. on the twenty-fifth she took a departure for the east, toward the British base at Algoa Bay (now Port Elizabeth) where the troops were to be disembarked. Her commander, Captain Robert Salmond, was anxious to make a quick passage and in order to minimize the travelling distance kept the ship close to the coast – too close in fact. The course he set took *Birkenhead* directly over a submerged reef two miles off aptly named Danger Point. In the darkness the vessel ran onto the hidden rocks, her hull was torn open and she sank 20 minutes later. It was the actions of those on board during these few minutes of grace that hugely excited the British public and gave rise to a legend.

Immediately after the vessel ran aground, the pumps were manned and the most strenuous efforts were made to clear away the ship's boats. *Birkenhead* was a side-wheel paddle steamer and her boats were of two basic types: she carried conventional boats slung in davits on the after section, but much of her life-saving capacity was vested in two paddle-box boats. Unorthodox, heavy and clumsy – each boat was stowed upside down in such a way that it formed part of the housing for the paddle wheels. During an emergency the difficulties associated with getting a paddle-box boat into the water could make it a liability as much as an asset. The invention of Captain G. Smith RN, they were labelled in 1846 by the naval correspondent of *The Times* as 'the most abominably ugly made

Patterns of Loss of Life in the Worst Survivable Wrecks of British Passenger Ships, 1850–1900*

Ship/year of loss	Passengers plus crew		Crew		Male passengers		Women/ children	
	On board	Lost	On board	Saved	On board	Saved	On board	Saved
Tayleur/1854	~630†	~340† (58%)	71	57	~360†	230	~200	1/2
Royal Charter/1859	~487‡	~446 (92%)	112	18	~286‡	23§	~100	none
Northfleet/1873	379	294 (78%)	37	10	243	71	46/53	2/2
Atlantic/1873	957	546 (58%)	146	89	531	323	167/116	1 child
Cospatrick/1874	479	476 (99%)	44	3	182	none	126/127	none
Kapunda/1887	314	298 (95%)	41	8	100	8	88/85	none
Utopia/1891	878‖	562 (64%)	59	24	667	~282	85/67	~5/~5¶
Total	~4124	~2962 (72%)	510	209 (41%)	~2369	~937 (39%)	~1260	~18 (1.5%)

*   A death toll of greater than 290 persons has been taken as the arbitrary threshold. Figures in parentheses give percentages of lives saved or lost. Wrecks that occurred in inland waterways, such as that of the pleasure steamer *Princess Alice* by collision on the Thames in 1878 (death toll ~635), and of the steamer *Wah Yeung* by fire on the Canton River in 1887 (likely death toll ~600) have not been included. The after hold of the *Wah Yeung* was said to have held at least 180 women, not one of whom escaped.

†   Possibly an upper limit. At the loss inquiry the vessel's owners stated that there were 485 adult passengers on board. The number of children on the vessel (~100 according to newpapers of the time) and the number lost seem not to appear in official figures.

‡   Total includes 11 riggers (shore-based ship-workers)

§   Total includes 5 riggers

‖   Total includes 3 stowaways

¶   Exact figures are unknown, *The Times* of 21 March 1891 reported 'very few women saved and virtually all children lost'.

boats ever built in modern times,' and in the same year their performance was severely criticised in the House of Commons.[4] In *Birkenhead*'s hour of need the paddle-box boats failed totally, despite relatively calm conditions prevailing at the time.

On board *Birkenhead* were about 618 troops and crew (there is some uncertainty as to the exact number, which varies depending on the source of the account), together with seven women and 13 children. As the ship settled rapidly by the head, Salmond ordered that the troops not helping with the pumps or attempting to launch the paddle-box boats should be formed up on the poop. Three conventional boats – two cutters and a gig – were launched successfully and Salmond had the women and children placed in one of the cutters. Almost immediately after the cutters had got away the ship began to break up. The bow broke off at the foremast and the funnel and yards crashed down on the starboard paddle-box boat, crushing many of those who were wrestling with davits frozen solid with rust. A second gig and the port-side paddle-box boat capsized as they were being launched. Throughout the carnage an extraordinary discipline governed the troops, who had been ordered to remain in their places by Major Seaton of the 74th Highlanders, the officer in overall charge.[5] There was no attempt to break ranks, and the safety of the women and children in the cutter was not compromised. Soon after the bow broke away, what was left of *Birkenhead* separated amidships and she, along with most of those still on board, disappeared beneath the surface of the sea. Captain E.W.C. Wright of the 91st, one of the few officers to survive, described the scene as one where 'the utmost order was observed by all on board, and until the vessel totally disappeared there was not a cry or murmur from soldiers or sailors.'[6] There were only 184 survivors, 116 of whom, including all 20 women and children, were rescued from the boats.

When news of the catastrophe reached Britain the behaviour of the steadfast troops on *Birkenhead* was widely admired. Lieutenant-General William Napier, a military historian of note, was among the many who voiced approval: his effusive sentiments that 'the occasion was great, was noble, was good, – the heroism never surpassed … it was the strong fount of military honour gushing up from the heart', not only reflected the national mood, but drew attention away from the deficiencies in the ship's management and safety equipment – and from the death toll of 454.[7] As Salmond and his officers had died in the wreck there was no need for the resulting inquiry to scrutinise their questionable navigation, or possible lack of maintenance of the boats. The enduring memory of *Birkenhead* soon became one of troops standing fast in the 'Birkenhead Drill', and with it the ideal of 'Women and children first!' was established.[8] Relatively few had been involved, but this fact was lost in the general euphoria. Importantly, the rigid discipline characterising the loss of the *Birkenhead* was rarely duplicated when ships of the merchant service came to grief.

As the pace of emigration from Britain quickened throughout the 1840s and 1850s, so too did the rate at which emigrant ships joined the long list of vessels wrecked or lost. Attracted by the high profits of the emigrant trade, shipowners often used vessels, so-called 'coffin ships', that were either unseaworthy or wholly unsuitable for the carriage of passengers. Conditions in the steerage could be atrocious, with emigrants left largely to their own devices for the duration of the voyage. In these circumstances 'it was scarcely possible to induce the passengers to be decent with respect to the common wants of nature', and the 'tween deck in which they were accommodated became 'like a loathsome dungeon'. When the hatches of such vessels were opened at the end of the passage it was said that 'the steam rose, and the stench was like that from a pen of pigs'.[9] 'Much misery and discomfort have I witnessed in crowded emigrant vessels,' wrote 'Old Voyager' in a letter to *The Times* of 18 January 1850, 'no other class of ships go to sea so badly found, for human freight is the least valuable of any consigned to the captain of a merchant ship.' This lack of worth was reflected in ship losses, for in the eight years from 1847 to 1854 no fewer than 70 British emigrant ships foundered, with several of the wrecks involving catastrophic loss of life.

Unseaworthy ships were not simply those that were decayed or overloaded. An inadequate crew (so-called unseaworthy seamen) or defective navigational equipment could also render a vessel unfit to proceed to sea. The *Tayleur* was deficient in both categories. Under stress of weather, and possibly because her compasses were not set up properly, this brand-new 1979-ton iron clipper was driven onto rocks in Dublin Bay on 21 January 1854. In the hours before the vessel struck, her less than competent crew could not be persuaded aloft to reduce sail – an operation which might have enabled her to be sailed clear. Unable to accept that British seamen could behave in such a way, the *Examiner* later reported that 'the ship was very badly manned by a motley crew of foreigners – Lascars, Chinese and French. These lubbers could neither make nor shorten sail; the business of taking in sail was … left to the wind, which did it after its peremptory fashion, by splitting and rending the maintopsail from the yard.'[10] However, the *Examiner*'s xenophobic reaction was completely unfounded as only 12 of *Tayleur*'s 71-man crew were 'foreigners'.

The *Tayleur* was bound for Melbourne from Liverpool with emigrants, and in what was a disorganised evacuation only about 290 of the 630 people on board managed to reach the shore. On being asked by passengers to lower the boats, *Tayleur*'s commander, Captain Noble, gestured toward the waves and said, 'What use?';[11] *Tayleur*'s boats were not launched. Most of those who survived reached safety by hauling themselves along ropes established between the ship and the shore – a feat requiring both physical strength and a ruthless outlook as crew members did little to assist the weak. Once on dry land, several seamen further disgraced themselves by making off without attempting to help those still on board. A cabin passenger reported: 'the most desperate struggles for life were made by the wretched passengers; great numbers of women jumped overboard in the vain hope of reaching land and the ropes were crowded by hundreds, who, in their eagerness, terror and confusion, frustrated each others efforts for self-preservation. Many of the women would get half way and then, unable to proceed further … would be forced from their hold [to fall to their deaths in the sea] by those who came after them.'[12] The circumstances of the disaster were such that even to save himself a man was not only pressed to the limit of endurance but needed good fortune as well. Women were fatally disadvantaged by a lack of upper body strength and the heavy-skirted and high-booted style of their clothing, which restricted free movement and became an impossible encumbrance once saturated with water. Of the nearly 200 women and children on the *Tayleur*, only one woman and two girls were saved – the latter by being carried ashore tied to the backs of men. The fact that the vessel's seamen survived in disproportionately large numbers – 57 of the 71 lived through the wreck – did little to improve public feeling toward them.

Incidents such as the loss of the *Tayleur* played their part in causing the British Parliament to introduce two complementary pieces of maritime legislation: the comprehensive Merchant Shipping Act of 1854 and the Passengers Act of 1855. The former was an ambitious attempt to regulate all aspects of ship management, equipment, manning, and navigation, while the latter gave the rules governing the carriage of passengers by sea. A specialised Marine Department of the Board of Trade, set up in 1850, became the administering authority. Much of the Passengers Act was concerned with apparently mundane matters – passenger ticketing, supply of foodstuffs, allocation of living space, and the like – but buried among its 103 clauses was one with dramatic consequences for passenger safety; this was the twenty-seventh clause, containing the regulations applying to ships' boats and other life-saving equipment.

Clause 27 became of great interest to thoughtful Victorians contemplating travel by sea. Most importantly, the clause specified that it was a passenger ship's tonnage, rather than the number of people on board, which governed the size and minimum number of boats the vessel should carry. This regulation led to extraordinary anomalies. A sailing ship of between 1000 and 1500 tons might be transporting between 450 and 600 people, but could comply with the law by carrying just six boats with the capacity to accommodate 170. In the event of disaster, only one person in three would be able to find a place in the boats. Sailing vessels in other tonnage classes were affected proportionately, and the similar tendency to crowd steamships with passengers meant that these too were poorly served with life-saving equipment. If the survival of those on board a sinking passenger ship were to depend solely on her own boats, at least two thirds were certain to be drowned. Under the provisions of Clause 27 it became inevitable that the places in lifeboats would be fought over. In this circumstance, of course, women and children were the biggest losers.

The details of these struggles for life were usually glossed over in contemporary accounts, but the English language newspaper *Buenos Ayres Standard* made an exception when reporting the burning of the (albeit Italian) steamship *America* in December 1871. A correspondent wrote:

The crew had escaped with a few of the passengers in the only available boat; the other five lifeboats could not be lowered, and it is even said they had not been lowered in years; ineffectual efforts were made to cut them loose from the davits … The flames rose so rapidly that in the panic no other means of safety could be found but such as planks or spars offered. We hear of deadly struggles with knives for even these frail supports, and life belts were snatched from the weak hands of women; revolvers were drawn, and two or three persons shot. Husbands perished trying to save their wives, children were drowned before the eyes of their parents … It was nothing but every man for himself. Life-buoys were snatched from frightened ladies, and there were bloody encounters among the men … It was a life and death struggle, in which brute strength alone availed. No consideration for age or sex. One fellow was seen to stab a woman and tear off her life belt.[13]

A frequently recurring theme in descriptions of such incidents was that boats were unusable because maintenance had been neglected. Often, as happened on the *America*, the telling command from the ship's captain was not 'Women and children first!' but 'Every man for himself!'

The obvious argument that a ship should carry no more passengers than the number of places available in her boats was for decades dismissed on economic grounds. Many shipowners were reluctant to concede deck space to life-saving equipment, and their views were well represented in Parliament – the greater the deck space, the more passengers a vessel could carry and the larger the profit. A letter to *The Times* of 3 September 1858 summed up this situation as one where 'the ship-owners of Great Britain are in many instances very charitable … but are very loath to adopt improvements on board their ships which would often be the means of saving life.' However, it was not simply a matter of providing passenger vessels with more boats. The safe working of a sailing ship depended on unhindered access to all of the hundreds of ropes used in sail handling, and this was impossible if boats cluttered the decks. The preferred mode of stowage was to have them slung in davits, but the layout of a sailing vessel's rigging and the closeness of her upper deck to the waterline admitted few places where davits could be positioned. If mounted on the upper deck, the boats they held became liable to storm damage. Often the only safe position was aft, on the vessel's poop if she had one, but usually with room for just one boat on either side. Others were carried in ways that made them much less accessible in an emergency. Frequently stowed upside down, they were lashed to beams raised above the upper deck (known as skids), and launching them was both labour-intensive and time-consuming. Boats stowed keel-up first needed to be turned upright, and as each craft weighed at least half a ton, and perhaps much more, this was no trivial matter on a rolling vessel. A further co-ordinated effort involving several sailors was required to get the boat hoisted up, swung over the side and placed in the water.

The solution to the ship's boat problem demanded not only a change in the philosophy concerning the number carried, but also technical improvements to the boats themselves and to the ways they were stowed and launched. While the Passengers Act of 1855 recognised the importance of equipping passenger vessels with 'lifeboats', it was remarkably vague in specifying what a lifeboat actually was – indicating only that it should be a ship's boat furnished with flotation aids (buoyancy tanks) and able to be launched quickly.

The craft on which so much reliance might be placed bore outlandish names: pinnace, longboat, jolly-boat, gig, launch, cutter, whaler, and dinghy. These designations reflected not only differences in size and construction, but in the ways the boats could be rigged for sail, and the number and seating arrangement of rowers. Possibly their most significant common feature, often to the detriment of those unlucky enough to find themselves in one (or lucky enough, depending on the point of view), was that they were open to the elements. In addition to the obvious risk of exposure, even short-term occupancy of a ship's boat could lead to severe constipation and the painful soft tissue infections known as salt-water boils. Occupancy was determined by the boat's 'cubical capacity', and, according to the Board of Trade, 15 cubic feet of 'cubical capacity' allowed 'sufficient room for one adult to sit'.[14] This formula did not take creature comfort into account, nor did it accurately reflect the number of people a boat could safely hold. When loaded to its rated capacity, a ship's boat was a distinctly uncomfortable place to be, with those crowded onto its hard wooden seating having little opportunity to move their limbs or stand. Continual exposure to sea-spray and the lively motion of the boat under most sea conditions added further dimensions to the misery.

Wooden boats were either carvel-built (having flush planking) or clinker-built (having overlapping planking), but both types were relatively fragile in the context of what might be expected from them in an emergency. Sturdy, riveted iron construction became increasingly fashionable after 1870 and large-scale experiments on collapsible boats were being carried out in 1875. Collapsibles had first been mooted in 1852 by the Reverend E.L. Berthon, of Fareham. They were made of rubberised canvas (or felt) supported on a wooden frame, but were nowhere near as seaworthy as conventional lifeboats. Their advantage lay in the fact that their stowage required much less deck space, and four were successfully used when the *Titanic* was abandoned in 1912. A boat's usefulness at a time of shipwreck depended not only on its design and construction but also on sea conditions, and, equally importantly, on the ability of its crew to manage it once it had been successfully launched.

The relationship between sailors and the passengers in their care could be put to the test when a vessel was abandoned. Passengers contributed little to a boat's management and occupied valuable space while consuming equally valuable provisions. It was therefore easy for sailors to regard them as so much deadweight. This perceived uselessness, often coupled with a clique-like camaraderie among the seamen, made polarisation into 'them' and 'us' factions almost inevitable. Passengers tended to become further marginalised if conditions in the boat worsened. In deteriorating weather they were regarded as a huge liability, more affected by temperature extremes than hardy seamen and likely to imperil the boat's stability. Sailors were needed to manage the boat, but passengers might be regarded as expendable.[15] It is an unfortunate fact that seamen were inclined to commandeer the boats as a passenger vessel was being abandoned.

The Board of Trade, which after 1854 was responsible for policing all matters relating to merchant shipping, required that boats were 'properly supplied with all requisites for use'. However, 'all requisites' meant only painter, oars, rowlocks, bottom plug, baler, rudder and tiller. As there was no requirement for boats to carry fresh water or provisions, occupants might find themselves unwitting participants in acts of survival cannibalism – a practice not uncommon prior to 1880, nor, in most maritime circles at least, seen to be reprehensible. Few questions were asked of Captain Archibald Wilson, who survived the sinking of his vessel *Perseverance* after it was 'cut through' by ice off the coast of Newfoundland in 1861. Wilson and his crew of nine left *Perseverance* in a boat with no provisions at all: 'had not time to get even a drop of water put into the boat, it happened so suddenly,' he said later.[16] One by one the sailors died from cold and starvation until Wilson alone was left. After 18 days he was picked up by the Bristol barque *Lord Petre*, having spent most of that time with just two corpses for company. His survival defies explanation unless it involved subsisting on the bodies of the dead. On many other occasions survivors freely admitted to eating the flesh of deceased companions. Since the practice was sanctioned as the last resort of shipwrecked sailors, only the most extreme cases – like that of the *Euxine* where murder was involved – attracted official attention. Sailors, probably the most maligned class of worker in British history, were not expected to behave in a civilised fashion. If their dietary habits fell below normally accepted standards this was seen to be in keeping with their general conduct, which was widely held to be uniformly bad.

Ships' boats therefore provided a tenuous lifeline for those unfortunate enough to find themselves on a vessel in distress during the nineteenth century. Although there was always the hope that a passing ship might render assistance, any such encounter would be entirely accidental. And even if another vessel did loom into view at the hour of need, this was no guarantee that she would stop. Indeed, for much of the era there was no compulsion, other than moral obligation, for her to do so. While an optimist on a sinking passenger ship might look on the lifeboats with a measure of hope, a pragmatist would view them with despair. Public dissatisfaction with the state of affairs brought about by the provisions of Clause 27 received regular expression in the columns of Britain's newspapers.

The inadequacies of boats and safety procedures on nineteenth-century passenger ships was never more clearly demonstrated than during a bitterly cold night in January 1873, when the 20-year-old Hobart-bound sailing vessel *Northfleet* was run down by a steamer off Dungeness. At the time of her sinking the 940-ton *Northfleet* was under the command of Captain Edward Knowles, and was carrying 342 emigrants and a crew of 37. Most of the male passengers were Irish 'navvies', being taken out under contract by the Tasmanian Main Line Railway Company, and many were accompanied by wives and children. Knowles' wife of six weeks, Fredericka, was also on board.

Northfleet's voyage was plagued from the outset. After sailing from London's East India Dock on 13 January 1873, her 'tween-decks were found to be so overcrowded that a number of passengers were disembarked on arrival at Gravesend. (Ironically, these fortunate few complained of being left behind to local magistrates.) Edward Knowles had been *Northfleet*'s chief officer, but, almost at the moment of departure from Gravesend on the seventeenth, was given command when her regular master was called ashore as a trial witness. The vessel proceeded into the English Channel, where several days were spent battling a southwesterly gale. Seasickness was so prevalent among the women that Knowles turned back to Dungeness to await more moderate weather. The accident occurred at 11 p.m. on 22 January, as the *Northfleet*, surrounded by other ships and exhibiting the correct lights for a vessel at anchor, lay in Dungeness Roads. Nearly everyone on board was asleep, and there was no warning that a collision was imminent. A steamer surged out of the night, struck *Northfleet* squarely amidships, and then backed away and disappeared in the darkness. It was a fatal blow. With her timbers below the waterline crushed and splintered, the emigrant ship began to sink almost immediately. In common with most other sailing vessels of her vintage, *Northfleet*'s hull was not divided into compartments by transverse bulkheads. The sea flooded in through the breach in her side – too rapidly to be cleared by the pumps.

Once it was realised the vessel was sinking, panic ensued. Those below 'streamed up on deck, half-dressed and almost mad with fright'. Rockets were fired off and blue lights burned on deck, but as there was no standard night signal for a vessel in distress, few on board the 200 or so ships in close proximity comprehended their purpose – it was simply assumed that *Northfleet* was energetically requesting the services of a pilot. The shore-based lifeboat at Dungeness also remained unlaunched.

There was little chance that the *Northfleet* would be abandoned in an orderly fashion, as passengers outnumbered crew members by nine to one. Many of the emigrants were still incapacitated by illness, as well as disoriented by the darkness and their unaccustomed surroundings. A perfunctory boat drill had been carried out by the Board of Trade before

'The Rush For The Boats'; the loss of the *Northfleet*. (*The Graphic*, 1873)

the vessel left Gravesend, but it was undertaken only to make sure that
Northfleet's lifeboats could be lowered. Board of Trade officials and the
ship's officers saw no need to familiarise the passengers with the life-saving
equipment, or to inform them about emergency procedures. According
to the Board of Trade, *Northfleet*'s six boats should have been able to safely
hold 142 people – five more than the statutory requirement for a passenger
vessel of her tonnage. In the event, only two boats were launched during
the 30 to 40 minutes it took for her to sink.

Knowles' first concern was for his wife. The two lifeboats held in davits
on the poop were cleared away and Fredericka Knowles was placed in
one under the care of John Easter, the ship's boatswain. The other four
boats were cutters, also stowed in the after part of the ship, but carried
bottom upwards on skids. It would have taken an organised group about
15 minutes to get just one of these upright and safely over the side. As it
was, *Northfleet*'s seamen had time only to cut their lashings, in the hope that

as the vessel sank they would float clear and offer support to people in the water. When the emigrants recognised that few of their number would be saved by the boats, disorder turned rapidly to chaos. As desperate men forced their way into the starboard quarter boat, Knowles drew a revolver and ordered them out, hoping to secure places for the women and children. When the men refused to move, Knowles motioned to the boatswain to stand clear and fired two shots. Thomas Biddiss, a steerage passenger who had seated himself near Fredericka Knowles, 'almost felt the first pass over his head' and, despite the second hitting him in the leg, remained where he was. Although the boatswain threatened to cut their hands off if they attempted to do so, others clambered into the boat when Knowles' revolver misfired. To the sound of continuous ringing of the alarm bell and the shrieks of those left on deck, the boat was then lowered away – becoming slightly stove-in during the process. The port quarter boat was also launched, apparently after being entirely taken over by men. Soon after the boats had pulled clear, the stricken ship sank in 70 feet of water, leaving only the topmasts projecting above the surface.

The Deal-based pilot cutter *Princess* and the Kingsdown lugger *Mary* were attracted to the scene and saved several people in the water, as well as others who had taken refuge in the vessel's upper rigging. The *City of London*, a passing steam-tug, also succeeded in picking up a number of people from the water, together with the occupants of the lifeboats. *Northfleet*'s decks were illuminated by distress flares up until the moment of her final plunge, and in the eerie light the rescuers had seen anguished parents holding children above their heads, begging for them to be saved. But of the 53 children on the vessel only two lived through the disaster. Just 85 of *Northfleet*'s complement of 379 survived the wintry conditions of the English Channel. Of the 46 women on *Northfleet*, Fredericka Knowles and one other were saved, but Captain Knowles went down with his ship. Thomas Biddiss, who was among the saved, achieved short-lived fame as 'the man shot by Captain Knowles'.

The vessel that had run down the *Northfleet* proved to be the Spanish steamer *Murillo*. Her movements in the hours following the collision attracted suspicion, and she was eventually tracked down to Cadiz. Fresh paint was found to be covering recently dented bow plates and log entries made at

The Captain's Farewell'; the loss of the *Northfleet*. (The *Illustrated London News*, 1873)

the time of the collision were patently false. Evidence given by two British engineers on *Murillo* confirmed her involvement. Her crew were taken into custody in Spain, and writs totalling £24,000 issued in Britain against her owners. A Spanish Admiralty Court sitting in June ordered that the master's certificate be cancelled for 12 months, but made no recommendation as to what should be the fate of the vessel. She continued to trade, but in September 1873 strayed into British territorial waters where she was arrested and detained. She was found to be in a generally decrepit state and her sale, on order of the British Admiralty High Court, realised just £7050.

The Board of Trade Inquiry into the loss of *Northfleet* concluded in December. Besides making obvious comments regarding *Murillo*'s mismanagement, and the callous and devious behaviour of her crew, the court drew particular attention to the deficiencies in *Northfleet*'s safety equipment, which had so contributed to the large death toll. Twelve life jackets had been on board but these failed to assist in saving a single life. Despite effective cork life jackets being available since at least 1854 it was not until 1890 that British passenger vessels were required to carry one for each person on board. The number of persons saved by *Northfleet*'s lifeboats is uncertain, but one had no more than 19 occupants when picked up, and the other probably less (each was rated as able to safely hold 30 adults). According to Biddiss, the starboard boat contained just nine persons, whereas John Easter, the more credible witness, gave the figure as 16.

The sinking of the *Northfleet* came at a time when revelations by Samuel Plimsoll were galvanising support for maritime reform. Plimsoll, MP for Derby from 1868 to 1880 and a campaigner for social justice, was so affected by the sight of four storm-wrecked vessels when on a short voyage in 1864 that he became determined to reduce loss of life at sea. At the end of this rough passage, the emotional Plimsoll fell weeping into the arms of his wife, who had been waiting apprehensively on the quay. She too was in tears, for neither had expected to see the other again.[17] As part of a protracted campaign to improve the lot of the British seafarer, Plimsoll wrote *Our Seamen – an Appeal*, which created a sensation when it appeared at the beginning of 1873. The book exposed many of the dubious practices associated with the merchant marine, and brought to the fore the important issue of seaworthiness, particularly in relation to the practices of overloading, over-insurance and the sending of vessels to sea in a badly decayed condition. It swayed popular opinion in favour of Plimsoll's 'Unseaworthy Ships Bill', which, although narrowly failing to gain the support of the House, contained many provisions that were eventually incorporated into the Merchant Shipping Act of 1875. This legislation famously caused 'Plimsoll's Line' to be painted on every ship's side and was certainly the most significant step toward preventing British shipowners from dangerously overloading their vessels.[18] Plimsoll's arguments were always backed by copious statistics, not all of which were entirely accurate, but he rarely overstated the number of lives lost at sea. During 1873 the lives of 3263 British seamen were lost (2231 by wreck and 1032 by accident) out of a work force of 208,000 – an annual mortality rate of 1.6 per cent.[19] Notwithstanding apparent improvements to safety and conditions brought about by the Merchant Shipping Act of 1875, the rate hovered around 2 per cent per annum well into the 1880s. The publication of *Our Seamen* and the loss of the *Northfleet* did much to heighten awareness of maritime safety in the early stages of 1873, but despite being urged to find ways to ensure passenger vessels were properly equipped with efficient boats, Plimsoll never turned his attention in this direction.

Public confidence in sea travel received a further setback in 1873. Just three months after the *Northfleet* disaster, news reached Britain that the White Star liner *Atlantic* had run aground with huge loss of life on the eastern seaboard of North America. The *Atlantic* was no elderly sailing vessel but a modern 3707 tons register four-masted iron steamship, less than two years old, and built, according to publicists, with 'care, forethought and constructive ingenuity in her planning and fitting out, equalled only by the lavish cost'.[20] She was equipped with five transverse bulkheads that 'divided the hull into six water-tight compartments', and her 10 lifeboats were capable of holding about 350 people.

Atlantic came to grief at a location she should never have been near. Eleven days after leaving Liverpool for New York with 811 passengers and a crew of 146, her captain, James A. Williams, realised that his ship was in danger of running out of fuel. At noon on 31 March 1873, when the steamer was 460 miles from her destination, an estimated 127 tons of coal remained in the bunkers – barely enough for her to complete the journey even under the most favourable conditions. Williams prudently turned the vessel's bow towards Halifax, Nova Scotia, believing it to be 170 miles to the north. Despite uncertainties in his ship's exact position, he turned in at midnight, and was still in his bunk when, at 3.15 a.m., *Atlantic* struck rocks off Mosher Island on Nova Scotia's south coast. Williams and his officers were deceived because they had underestimated both their vessel's speed and the strength of a westerly setting current. As a result, *Atlantic* was 12 to 13 miles off course when she ran full tilt onto the shore. Her seamen were keeping such a poor lookout they failed to observe a lighthouse to the east, even though it was readily visible. The first warning of danger came with the lookout's cry of '*Breakers ahead!*'[21]

Atlantic's 'water-tight' compartments availed her little and within minutes of running ashore she began to fall over onto her port side. As the decks inclined toward the vertical it became virtually impossible for people still below to find an exit – only those first to the ladders had time to reach the upper deck; passengers who stopped to dress or paused to gather up children had little chance to escape. A few – probably no more than 20 – managed to scramble through portholes and onto the ship's side, where the starboard rigging provided a temporary refuge. Third Officer Cornelius Brady and two quartermasters, Edward Owens and John Speakman, established a line between the fore-part of the ship and a large rock about 40 yards distant, and by this means about 200 people – mainly those who had immediately come on deck after the vessel struck – made their way to the seaweed-covered rock and precarious safety. Other ropes were set up between the rock and the island and, by their aid, and with assistance from another quartermaster, Robert Thomas, some 50 persons were transferred through the surf to the shore. Many others, too numbed by the biting cold to keep a hold on the lifelines, died in the attempt. Brady trekked inland to alert the island community to the unfolding tragedy and by 6 a.m. three local fishing boats, which had to be carried across the island to their launching point, began the difficult rescue.

Those who had taken refuge in the rigging were faced with a fearful dilemma – either to make their way forward to the lifelines and risk being washed overboard, or remain clinging to the shrouds in the hope of being rescued by the fishing boats before succumbing to exposure. Only the most hardy survived. One passenger trapped in the rigging for seven hours saw able-bodied men gradually give way and fall to their death. Rescue efforts continued until two o'clock in the afternoon when Chief Officer J.W. Firth was hauled into a boat from his perch in the mizzen shrouds. Firth had entered the rigging after *Atlantic* heeled over, and at dawn counted 32 others in the same predicament, including one woman. By noon he and the woman were all who remained, but she died soon after, 'her half-nude body … still fast in the rigging, her eyes protruding, her mouth foaming, a terrible ghastly spectacle, rendered more horrible by contrast with the numerous jewels which sparkled on her hands.'[22] Firth was the last person to be saved; 546 had lost their lives, but 411 survived. Of the 167 women (three of whom were stewardesses) and 116 children, only 12-year-old John Hindley (or Linley) lived through the disaster.

In an outspoken analysis of the wreck, the *New York Herald* described *Atlantic*'s Liverpool crew as 'one of the hardest gathered into any vessel' and

– notwithstanding the heroism of Owens, Speakman, Brady, and Thomas
– accused the seamen, 89 of whom survived, of being 'a bad lot' who had
plundered and abused the dead. Not without cause the newspaper assigned
blame, both to the White Star Line for its parsimony in supplying *Atlantic*
with coal, and to Captain Williams for being asleep as his vessel approached
a treacherous coastline – offering the opinion on 6 April 1873 that 'Captain
Williams, who now lounges about the principal hotel in Halifax, is the man
who is responsible, and ought to dangle from the yard arm before the rising
of another sun.' Less controversial was the *Herald*'s statement that *Atlantic*'s
boats had proved 'utterly and entirely useless – might as well have been left
behind.' The port-side boats had washed away soon after the vessel ran
aground, and one starboard-side boat, containing about 40 men, capsized
as it was being launched. All its occupants drowned, including Second
Officer H.J. Metcalfe, senior officer of the watch at the time the ship was
run ashore. Metcalfe's failure to ensure that a proper lookout was being kept
would have called for censure had he lived.

Most survivor reports suggest that once *Atlantic* had begun to list to port
the remaining starboard side boats became unusable. One eyewitness did,
however, speak of them as being 'taken possession of by men and several
cast off', but whatever happened they were totally unsuccessful in saving
life. Given the nature of the disaster little could be done to help any of the
passengers, let alone the women and children. 'Everything happened so
quickly,' said one survivor; 'before the strongest had got out of the choked
passageways, the females were either so bewildered, or the water had so
impeded their progress, that very few came on deck. Those who did were
swept away before they could fasten themselves [to the rigging] or be
secured by others.'[23]

Reacting to the maritime disasters of early 1873, Captain J.R. Ward RN,
Inspector of Lifeboats to the Royal National Lifeboat Institution (RNLI),
and in a position to know, expressed the view that 'there is no such thing
in use in our Merchant Service as a lifeboat worthy of the name.' Ward
cited insufficient buoyancy as the main defect and commented: 'better there
should be no lifeboats at all than that passengers at sea should suppose that
the boats provided for them were *bona fide* lifeboats, when in reality they
were only sham ones.'[24] In one sense, Ward was measuring the abilities of

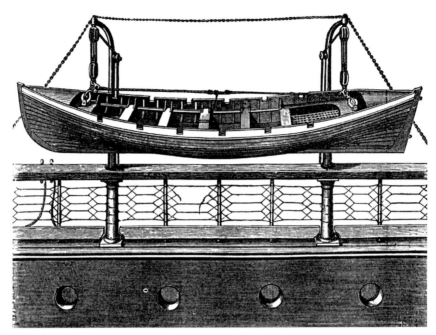

A ship's boat suspended in radial davits equipped with conventional falls. Although largely superseded by other davit types early in the twentieth century, radials remained in common use on small vessels up until the Second World War.

(G.S. Nares, *Seamanship*, 1882)

ships' boats against those of the larger shore-based lifeboats of the RNLI whose development was actively fostered, but he was aware that progress was being made. In 1872 he had been a member of a judging panel in a competition organised by the Society of Arts (later the Royal Society of Arts) to find a ship's boat which combined buoyancy and resistance to capsize, with strength and simplicity of use. Forty-four designs were submitted, with Woolfe & Son of London winning the prize for the best wooden boat, and Hamilton & Co. of Liverpool the prize for the best iron boat. Both boats were double-ended, 25 feet long and 7 feet wide, self-baling, and, even when swamped and full of people, buoyant enough to float with the gunwale about one foot above the surface of the water. Because the air cases in each boat were arranged to fit snugly along the sides, water that came in over the gunwale was kept well to the boat's centre, where it acted as ballast instead of slopping about and adding to the risk of capsize. Hamilton & Co. lifeboats soon found favour with shipbuilders, and represented an important landmark in the quest to improve safety at sea.

As much as the supply of efficient lifeboats was a problem, so were the difficulties of launching them without mishap. Where fitted, davits were usually of the radial type. Shaped like inverted fishhooks and arranged in pairs, the boats they held could be positioned either inboard and protected from the sea, or outboard and ready for immediate use. Falls – block and tackle arrangements attached to the davit heads – were used to lower the boats into the sea. At least four seamen were needed with this system – two on the ship's deck to control the tackle as the boat was being lowered, and two in the boat to unhook the falls once it was in the water. But boats held in radial davits could rarely be lowered from the uppermost side of a heavily listing ship; and, as a sinking vessel did not always settle on an even keel, 50 per cent of the available life-saving capacity might soon become useless. There were other problems, not least being the ease with which boats could be stove-in or capsized when launched into heavy seas. The degree of hazard was greatly increased if one fall was unhooked before the other, as the boat would almost certainly overturn when the released end dropped into the trough of a wave. Some believed that good seamanship could overcome the difficulties. One such was Lieutenant A.F. Kynaston RN, who, in 1846, offered the quaintly phrased but sensible advice that 'the falls must be lowered simultaneously and the tackles unhooked together; the boats must not be over-crowded by a motley crew, or the duty impeded and the dangers increased, as they often may be, by the confusion of hands and voices'.[25] But skilled sailors with the ability to keep their wits about them at a time of crisis formed only part of the solution to the boat-launching problem.

By the middle of the nineteenth century, the basic davit-and-fall system could be modified in ways that decreased the risk of capsize. Charles Clifford's 'Patent Boat Lowering Gear' (1853) not only allowed a boat to be lowered evenly to the water without assistance from those on deck, but also enabled both falls to be released simultaneously. One person in the boat could operate the apparatus. Clifford's mechanism was significant for another reason: no matter how desperate the situation on the parent vessel, those left behind could not easily disrupt the lowering process.

Like Samuel Plimsoll, Clifford believed that loss of life at sea was largely preventable and much of his life was devoted to developing and proving the device. Also like Plimsoll, he was suspicious of the Board of Trade's ability to adjudicate on matters of maritime safety; both men viewed the organisation as corrupt and poorly managed. Writing in 1859, Clifford expressed his conviction that 'a great and selfish indifference to life obtains amongst all those connected with mercantile affairs.'[26] He saw apathy not only among the officials and maritime surveyors of the Board of Trade who declined to enforce safety regulations, but also among owners and ships' officers who failed to insist that their vessels were supplied with adequate life-saving equipment. 'Many,' he wrote, 'would submit to seeing their men drowned before their eyes without a murmur or a remonstrance.' Clifford backed his invention by challenging 'any six sailors by the present system of blocks, tackles and hooks to a trial against me – a landsman, singlehanded – to lower and entirely free from the ship a boat laden with any freight … and with the vessel going at any speed.'[27] This confidence was justified by notable successes – such as that in 1861 when four boats fitted with his apparatus were safely lowered from the sinking passenger steamer *Canadian*. A fifth boat not equipped with lowering gear capsized on launching, causing all on board to be drowned. Clifford's device, however, soon came into bitter competition with a boat-disengaging mechanism patented in 1857 by Captain C.M. Kynaston RN. Promoted under the name 'Life Hooks', Kynaston's apparatus similarly allowed both falls to be released as one, but left control of the lowering process with those remaining on deck.

In 1861 attempts by Kynaston's widow to show that her late husband's invention had achieved the greater degree of acceptance, merely produced confirmation that support for Clifford's was widespread, and that it was being fitted in a ratio of twenty to one over 'Life Hooks'. Indeed, at this time Clifford's gear was in general use on merchant vessels and was standard equipment on about 350 ships of the Royal Navy. Ten years later this situation had reversed somewhat, for while Clifford's device was still preferred by many major British shipping companies, Kynaston's had found favour on Her Majesty's vessels. According to Clifford's brother, in a caustic letter to *The Times* of 4 April 1872, this was due to influence exerted by the late Captain Kynaston's brother-in-law, who happened to be Controller of the Royal Navy. Other factors may well have contributed, however: an Admiralty committee appointed to 'Inquire into the Best

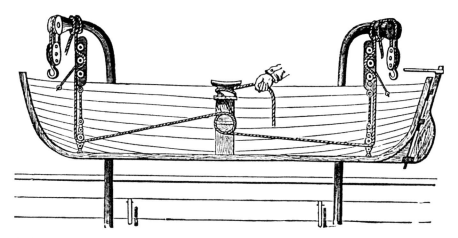

A diagrammatic representation of Charles Clifford's 'Patent Boat Lowering Gear' (1853). Clifford's contrivance had its faults – it occupied valuable space, the lowering pendants were susceptible to accelerated wear through chafing, and conventional falls (also shown) were needed to recover the boat. Not amenable to further development, the apparatus remained in general use until the mid-1880s. (G.S. Nares, *Seamanship*, 1882)

An alternative to Clifford's device, Sweeting's 'Boat Lowering and Disengaging Apparatus' also allowed those in the boat to control the lowering process. A drum brake on the ship's bulwark was used to regulate the rate of descent. (*The Mariner's Universal Gazette*, 1872)

Mode of Lowering Boats and Saving Life at Sea' reported in June 1872 that both devices had their faults, with Clifford's being particularly suspect because the lowering mechanism had a tendency to jam.[28] Many in the merchant service held similar reservations; the Peninsular & Oriental Steam Navigation Co. had no use for the devices, while William Inman, owner of the well-known Inman Line 'City' steamers, although believing that 'no apparatus matches the old principle of block and tackle', deferred to public opinion and equipped his ships with Clifford's.[29]

The New Zealand Government also deferred to public opinion in this matter. Every year throughout the 1870s its British-based administrators despatched scores of emigrant ships to the colony, with each being required to carry at least one boat equipped with Clifford's 'Patent Boat Lowering Gear'. It was by this regulation that the port lifeboat of the *Cospatrick* came to be fitted with Clifford's apparatus shortly before she departed from London for Auckland with emigrants on 11 September 1874. The maritime disasters of 1873 had failed to bring about change to the legislation governing ships' boats, and the six carried by the *Cospatrick* fully complied with the legal requirements of the time. Compliant or not, they were to prove woefully inadequate when the vessel came to a violent end 67 days after leaving Gravesend. Even so, had *Cospatrick*'s port lifeboat not been fitted with Clifford's gear, her fate would never have been known.

4. A FATAL VOYAGE

For what is the array of the strongest ropes, the tallest spars and the stoutest canvas against the mighty breath of the infinite, but thistle stalks, cobwebs and gossamer?

Mirror of the Sea, Joseph Conrad, 1906

During her time in the East India Export Dock in August 1874, the *Cospatrick* was loaded with a cargo of 992 tons deadweight consigned to Auckland. Britain had assumed sovereignty over New Zealand some 34 years earlier, and *Cospatrick*'s freight reflected the fact that the country's manufacturing capacity was still virtually non-existent. Termed a 'colonial cargo', the consignment included 257 tons of railway iron, large volumes of spirits, wine and beer, and quantities of varnish, turpentine, pitch, and vegetable oil (linseed and colza). Also loaded were articles that might be found in any well-stocked general store of the time – agricultural implements, haberdashery, medical supplies, crockery, furniture, tools, books, clothing, and children's toys. While this cargo was

FREE EMIGRATION TO NEW ZEALAND.

FREE PASSAGES are granted by the Government of New Zealand as under:

To Married and Single AGRICULTURAL LABOURERS, NAVVIES, PLOUGHMEN, SHEPHERDS MECHANICS &c.; also to Single FEMALE DOMESTIC SERVANTS, as Cooks, Housemaids, Nurses, General Servants, Dairy Maids, &c.

For terms and conditions, apply personally or by letter to the Agent-General for New Zealand 7 Westminster Chambers, London, S.W.

Advertisement encouraging emigration to New Zealand. (*Montrose, Arbroath and Brechin Review*, 1875)

being taken in, carpenters converted *Cospatrick*'s 'tween deck to emigrant accommodation. The 'tween deck, like the lower hold beneath it, extended over the full length of the vessel uninterrupted by bulkheads except for a section at the bow, 15 to 20 feet in length, where ship's stores were kept. The space was first divided into three compartments; bunks, mess tables and seats were added, ventilation was improved, and kitchens and privies set up; a small area was also partitioned off for use as a hospital. As the additions would be redundant once the *Cospatrick* reached Auckland, they were constructed of soft pine-wood, the cheapest timber available. The compartments created by the carpenters had a combined area of 5600 square feet – roughly equivalent to that of half a dozen small houses – but would accommodate more than 430 people for the duration of the voyage. Following the formula adopted on other emigrant ships, moral standards would be maintained, or would be seen to be maintained, by having single men berthed in the forward section, families amidships, and single women aft. Children were judged to have made the transition to adulthood on reaching 12 years of age and were housed separately from parents and younger siblings.

Sufficient provisions were laid in to allow for a non-stop passage to Auckland *via* the Cape of Good Hope. As *Cospatrick*'s water tanks were inadequate for a voyage of this length, the shortfall would be met by a Graveley's coal-fuelled distillation plant mounted on the upper deck. When operated efficiently this apparatus produced 23 gallons of fresh water per hour from sea water. In spite of the vessel carrying a Downton fire-pump in a fixed mounting on the forecastle, the New Zealand despatching officer, Edward A. Smith, ordered that a portable unit with 125 feet of delivery hose was also required. This addition effectively doubled the vessel's fire-fighting capability. Downton pumps were manually operated and, although difficult to maintain, were relatively efficient. Cranked enthusiastically by a crew of four, a 7-inch Downton, would deliver 40 gallons of water per minute onto a fire.[1] The ship was also equipped with 14 fire-buckets, all fitted with lanyards 'sufficiently long to draw water from the poop'. Better than nothing, these had an unfortunate tendency to float rather than fill when dropped into the sea.

Cospatrick's six boats were the minimum permissible for a vessel of her tonnage. A cutter and a launch were stowed on skids forward, and a longboat and the captain's gig on skids between the poop and the main-mast. Two lifeboats, clinker built, $24^1/_2$ feet in length and double-ended, were suspended in radial davits on the ship's quarters. All the boats were carried upright, except the longboat which was stowed keel up. A survey by Messrs James Boult and Samuel Cornish of the Board of Trade assessed their combined 'cubical capacity' to be 2747 cubic feet. Accordingly, they were rated as able to provide places for a total of 183 people – 13 more than the minimum allowable. On Edward Smith's instructions, shipwrights fitted Clifford's 'Patent Boat Lowering Gear' to the port lifeboat. Twelve life jackets and eight new lifebuoys completed the vessel's life-saving equipment.

In late August the men, women and children destined to be taken out as emigrants on the *Cospatrick* made their way to the New Zealand Emigration Depot at Blackwall on the Thames. Coming from all points of the British Isles, they represented a sector of the population described

A 7-inch Downton pump in a fixed mounting. This example is fitted in the lower deck of HMS *Warrior* at Portsmouth.

at the time as 'the agricultural poor'. Adult members of the group were mainly male farm labourers and female domestic servants. The New Zealand Government valued both classes of worker, and suitable applicants were provided with free passages. Young Irish and Scots women were particularly encouraged to emigrate as New Zealand endeavoured to correct a gender imbalance in its population. Migrant recruitment was by way of a scheme set up by the country's Agent-General in Britain, Isaac Featherstone, whose representatives – mainly local businessmen in key locations throughout Britain – received 15 shillings for each statute adult signed up.[2] The system was better suited to delivering quantity rather than quality; in 1874 many of those who arrived in the colony claiming to be farm workers were found to be 'but the mere off-scourings of the towns', said to care little for work, either in their home country or their adopted one.[3]

The final stage of the journey to the depot was made by way of the London & Blackwall Railway, described in a contemporary report as having 'some of the dirtiest and shabbiest stations and carriages to be found anywhere.'[4] Possibly because of the state of the carriages, but certainly contributing toward it, many of the farm workers travelled while still wearing 'earth-stained suits of fustian or corduroy'. As they emerged from the dingy confines of the Blackwall terminus they saw before them 'a grand bend in the river, alive with a crowd of red-sailed barges and other craft, through which a few big ships proceeded slowly'.[5] The sight induced apprehension as well as expectation, for many were well aware of the dangers that lay ahead. During June 1874 (the most recent month for which such information was freely available), no fewer than 58 British sailing vessels and four steamships had been lost through wreck, while another was reported as missing.[6] Somewhat countering this gloomy picture was the fact that of the more than 100 emigrant ships despatched by the New Zealand Government in the preceding 12 months, only the *Surat* had failed to arrive safely. Run ashore on the Otago coast by a drunken captain on 1 January 1874, the *Surat* became a total loss, but providentially all 271 emigrants and 37 crew survived.

The Blackwall Depot had opened on 11 May 1874. Built as the Brunswick Hotel some 70 years earlier, it stood at the western end of

The New Zealand Emigration Depot at Blackwall. During the 1870s the depot was a point of departure for thousands of New Zealand-bound emigrants. (*P.L.A. Monthly*, November 1929)

the Brunswick wharf. The depot's proximity to the East India Docks was administratively convenient, and the establishment was large enough to allow all emigrants assigned to a particular vessel to be gathered together under the one roof – intending settlers were thus saved from having to fend for themselves in 'waterside low lodging-houses ... of a strange and treacherous city', while waiting for ships that were often delayed.[7] The building had seen better days. Originally established to cater for wealthy travellers waiting for a passage to the East Indies, the Brunswick soon came into favour with the Duke of Clarence. The Duke, who succeeded to the throne in 1830 as William IV and who disliked the rigid formality of court, frequented the hotel in order to enjoy the relaxed company provided by East Indiamens' officers. Cabinet ministers later held ministerial functions in the large lower-floor dining room, which commanded broad views across the Thames Reaches to both the southeast and southwest. (After the Brunswick was converted to an emigration depot, this 'dining and keeping room' could seat 350.) On the parapet above the eastern end of the hotel's sweeping bow-windowed frontage, the longitude of Greenwich – the prime meridian – had been carved into the stonework under the direction of the Astronomer Royal. Guests delighted in being given rooms where they could sleep with their heads in the Eastern Hemisphere and their feet in the West (or vice versa). The hotel was also famous for its seafood cuisine; a contemporary poem by Thomas Love Peacock recorded:

> *At fam'd Blackwall, O Thames! upon thy shore,*
> *Where Lovegrove's tables groan beneath their store;*
> *We feasted on every famous dish,*
> *Dress'd many ways, of sea and river fish -*
> *Perch, mullet, eels and salmon, all were there,*
> *And whitebait, daintiest of our fishy fare ...*[8]

Lovegrove was the landlord who, in 1837, had leased the premises from its owners, the East India Dock Company.[9]

But in 1874 the basement kitchens of the old hotel were producing more basic fare for a very different clientele. At any one time, emigrants by the hundred might be waiting for their ship.[10] They were divided into 'messes' of eight or ten, each having its separate mess captain who, once the odour of cooking filled the air at dinnertime, 'kept his nose steadily pointed towards the door through which the smell came'[11]. On receiving a signal each 'captain' would descend into the kitchens, to return – often with a huge grin on his face, according to one visitor – bearing a large brown dish divided down the middle, with one half containing potatoes and the other, for a mess of eight, a steaming six-pound joint of roast beef. Bread, butter and condiments were liberally provided and, in deference to the many Scots emigrants who passed through the depot, oatmeal might be taken instead of tea. The food was far better than many were accustomed to.

Although their stay at the depot might last several days, the emigrants were housed and fed at the expense of the New Zealand Government, apart from a 'bedding-money' charge of £1 each for those over 12, and 10 shillings each for those under that age. The establishment was in the charge of a Mr and Mrs Watson – master and matron – who, by way of introduction to conditions on New Zealand-bound ships, imposed a regime similar to that the intending settlers would experience once at sea. Because space was at a premium, all were accommodated in packed dormitories – said to prepare them for the overcrowding they would endure on the voyage out. The largest room set aside for the single men could sleep 92. They were berthed in bunks, just 22 inches wide and arranged in pairs one over the other. Mattresses were stuffed with coconut fibre – a filling selected by virtue of the unwashed bodies that rested on it because it was believed (probably mistakenly) not to harbour lice. The largest family dormitory was able to sleep up to 20 couples and their children, with privacy maintained only by a screen of coarse (but 'neat patterned') curtain material hung across each bunk. Mingling of the sexes was discouraged to the greatest extent that the crammed living spaces would allow; both single women's dormitories were kept under lock and key, while the women themselves were not only chaperoned (the matron selected for this duty would also travel out with them) but took their meals in a separate dining room.[12]

Cospatrick's emigrants were inspected at the depot by the ship's surgeon, James F. Cadle, who turned away any showing signs of infectious disease. At 32 years of age, Cadle, whose home was near Newent in Gloucestershire, had twice journeyed to the Antipodes. On the second voyage he went to Otago as surgeon-superintendent on the New Zealand Shipping Company's *Dunfillan* – 'a sweet pretty ship and a good traveller' – with emigrants in 1873. During the 80-day voyage there had been just one death – that of an elderly woman from heart failure – and *Dunfillan*'s 163 surviving passengers were landed at Port Chalmers in good spirits: 'a healthier and happier looking lot having not been seen in the colony for a very long time indeed.'[13] This successful outcome was no doubt due as much to the rapidity of the passage as to Cadle's skill and dedication.

Surgeons on New Zealand-bound emigrant ships were paid by results – and self-interest, if not professional pride, dictated that they should keep their charges fit and well. Cadle was employed by the New Zealand Agent-General rather than Shaw, Savill & Co., and his contract promised a lump sum payment of £50 and a return of 10 shillings for each statute adult landed safely at Auckland.[14] He had accepted the post on *Cospatrick* reluctantly – a deciding factor being that it would enable him to visit a brother settled in New Zealand. Once the voyage was over he intended to enter into private practice ashore. The colonial view of surgeons and

Alexander and Henrietta Elmslie. (*The Graphic*, 1875)

surgeon-superintendents on emigrant ships was that they were men of low calibre, being 'with few exceptions, drunken, licentious or incompetent'.[15] Likewise, the prestigious medical journal *The Lancet* observed that the travelling public considered the ship's doctor as 'the ruck of the profession, whose capacities lay much more in the direction of brandy-and-water than the healing of the sick'.[16] Whatever the merits of these judgements, Cadle's actions on the *Cospatrick* would demonstrate that he came from a very different mould.

Cospatrick, with a crew of 44, cleared customs at the East India Docks on 8 September. The vessel remained under the command of 39-year-old Alexander Elmslie who, with wife Henrietta, maintained a home in Fairfield Road, Charlton, near Woolwich. The couple had three young children – daughters Jean and Jessie, and a son named for his father. Aberdeen born, Elmslie had come up through the ranks of Duncan Dunbar's fleet, gaining much of his early sea experience on the East Indiaman *Albuera* under the captaincy of his elder brother, James Aberdour Elmslie. A fellow master mariner reported him to be 'a good man, able, and every inch a sailor'.[17] Elmslie affected a substantial beard which doubtless enhanced this impression of seamanly competence. Before being made master of

| NEW ZEALAND.—The PASSENGERS' LINE.— |||||
Ships.	Tons.	Ports.		To Sail.
Cospatrick	2,000	Auckland	.. ..	Aug. 31
Glenlora	1,400	Auckland	.. ..	Sept. 10
Warwick	2,000	Auckland	.. ..	Sept. 30
Langstone	1,500	Wellington	.. ..	Sept. 5
Avalanche (new)	2,000	Wellington	.. ..	Sept. 25
City of Vienna	1,800	Wellington	.. ..	Oct. 5
Crusader	1,800	Canterbury	.. ..	Sept. 15
Lady Jocelyn	3,000	Canterbury	.. ..	Oct. 10
Hudson	1,400	Canterbury	.. ..	Oct. 25
Florence	1,500	Otago ..	.. ..	Aug. 28
Janet Cowan	2,000	Otago ..	.. ..	Sept. 20
W. E. Gladstone.. ..	1,000	Nelson ..	.. ..	Aug. 31
Anazi	1,200	Nelson .	.. ..	Sept. 15

The abovenamed ships are all first-rate passenger packets, fitted and equipped upon plans founded upon long experience.—Shaw, Savill, and Co., 34. Leadenhall-street, London.

N.B. To be obtained from the above, the 12th edition of the New Zealand Handbook with supplement, post free, 1s.

Final sailing notice for the *Cospatrick*, published in London on 28 August 1874. Other vessels on the list also met a violent end: *Avalanche* sank with the loss of 99 of the 102 people on board following a collision in 1877, while *Glenlora* and *Hudson* were sunk by U-boats during the First World War. *Anazi* and *Langstone* were fortunate to survive serious shipboard fires. (*The Times*, 1874)

the *Cospatrick* he had commanded the auxiliary sailing ship *Sea King*, and before her the *Marlborough*. He took over the *Sea King* in 1866 and in the same year ferried the vessel to Africa following her purchase by the Sultan of Zanzibar.[18] Jean, the eldest of the Elmslie children, was born at sea in 1866, most probably on *Sea King*; Henrietta Elmslie was therefore no stranger to the sea and had accompanied her husband on other voyages. In September 1874 Henrietta placed both daughters in the Belle Vue Boarding School at Herne Bay, Kent, and with four-year-old Alexander joined the *Cospatrick* for the voyage to New Zealand.

On the morning of 9 September the emigrants were embarked from the Brunswick Wharf. Four fare-paying male passengers also joined the ship before she proceeded down the Thames to moorings at Gravesend. As the vessel lay at the buoys on the tenth she was inspected by Captain John Forster RN, Emigration Officer to the Board of Trade. After satisfying himself that the ship's safety equipment and cargo complied with regulations, Forster pronounced her ready to go to sea. The Reverend J. Gadsun, a chaplain of the Thames Church Mission, also visited the ship at this time. Greatly impressed by the number of emigrants who attended his church services, he handed out schoolbooks and bibles to all and sundry. Although *Cospatrick*'s sailors were eating a meal when he stopped by the forecastle, they gave him a warm welcome. Gadsun was well acquainted with one of their number, having previously involved him in a long discussion on the subject of infidelity. He found the single male emigrants to be 'especially civil and steady', and noted that, at least in his presence, they did not gamble or swear.[19]

Although there was nothing about the ship's outward appearance to cause concern, a few passengers inexplicably refused to sail and took their luggage ashore. Likewise, a seaman expected to join the ship at the last moment unaccountably failed to turn up. There had earlier been a more definite feeling of foreboding: Henry McDonald's wife Jane had come from Montrose to be with him while the *Cospatrick* was fitting out in the East India Dock, and McDonald later observed that the two had never previously parted 'with such an indefinable sense of impending evil' than when she left to catch the train back to Scotland.[20]

Cospatrick sailed from Gravesend (a disquieting name for a port of departure) on the last of the flood tide at 5 a.m. on 11 September 1874. It was not an hour that favoured elaborate farewells and most passengers were still in their bunks when the mooring was slipped. On board were 479 people, of whom 429 – 178 men, 125 women and 126 children (16 of whom were infants) – were assisted emigrants. Dover was passed on the 12th and the vessel spent the night at anchor in the Downs. When she was off the Isle of Wight on the 13th letters were sent ashore, among them notes from the most senior and junior of her seamen. Alexander Elmslie wrote to inform his owners that all was well on board, while the letter 14-year-old Ordinary Seaman Hubert Attwell sent to his parents told of his excitement at being at sea for the first time.[21] The English coast was last in view on the 14th when the ship took a final departure from Start Point and set her bow into the Atlantic.

As the *Cospatrick* clawed her way southwards in the face of adverse winds, the emigrants gained their sea-legs and grew accustomed to their new surroundings; rural constitutions slowly adapted to the often disagreeable atmosphere of the packed 'tween deck spaces and the peculiarly unsettling motion of a tall ship in a seaway. To help run the

The *Cospatrick* at Gravesend. (*The Graphic*, 1875)

community in his charge, Cadle had appointed cleaners, watchmen and constables, a nurse, and cooks' assistants from the ranks of the emigrants. The watchmen kept guard over the hatchways at night, a duty which was overseen by the constables. The constables were also expected to inform the surgeon of any violation of the rules concerning smoking below decks, indecent acts, fighting, gambling, swearing, and drunkenness – in fact of any behaviour offensive to Victorian sensibilities. Cadle also supervised the ship's 'schoolmaster', Robert Fitzgerald, who was under contract to give lessons to *Cospatrick*'s emigrant children aged between five and 14 years. Instruction was to be provided, 'weather permitting, for not less than two hours after breakfast and two hours after dinner daily, Sundays excepted'.[22] Fitzgerald, a married emigrant from Cork, was also required to give two hours of religious instruction on Sundays, and to provide schooling for the single men at times: 'that must not interfere with the school hours of the children'.[23] For his efforts he expected to receive a gratuity of £5 on arrival at Auckland. The 'special constable' appointed by Cadle to clean out *Cospatrick*'s water-closets expected the same.

Much of the emigrants' time was spent either cleaning their living quarters or helping the cook prepare meals from the preserved foods on which their diet was based.[24] Clothes could be laundered in salt water twice weekly, and hung out in the rigging to dry. On Sundays the ship's complement was mustered on the upper deck and inspected by Cadle and Elmslie, one of whom would read Divine Service afterwards. The upper deck was an area where emigrants could at least stretch their legs, but even here strict segregation by gender was maintained: a father wishing to speak with his unmarried daughter could do so only from long range – while standing on the deck as she leaned across the poop rail above him.

The tedium was broken by the traditional visit from King Neptune when the equator was crossed, and by the occasional dance or concert organised by the emigrants themselves. Tensions in the congested 'tween deck spaces could lead to dispute – and dispute to violence – but except for minor lapses in discipline by two of their number, *Cospatrick*'s emigrants were well behaved.[25] At night the single men unobtrusively played cards, their game illuminated by light from a safety lantern at the hatchway entrance to their compartment. Identical glass-windowed lanterns, 'Price's Hexagonal Safety Candle Lanthorns', were placed at the other hatchways. They were lit at dusk by the 19-year-old emigrants' steward, Robert Godliaton, who carefully locked each one and kept the key. Regulations laid down in an 1864 Queen's Order in Council demanded that strict fire-safety procedures should be followed. Smoking and naked lights were forbidden below decks, and on many ships it was mandatory for emigrants to 'deliver up whatever lucifer matches they may have about them' on pain of punishment.[26] *Cospatrick*'s constables and watchmen were required to rigorously enforce the rules relating to naked lights and smoking, and the ship's galley fires were allowed to be alight only between 8 a.m. and 7 p.m. Despite these measures, fire-safety awareness on the vessel did not extend to fire drills, nor were boat drills considered a priority. The only exercise involving the boats occurred when Captain Elmslie's hat was blown overboard and, amidst great excitement among the emigrants, the port lifeboat – the one equipped with Clifford's 'Patent Boat Lowering Gear' – was despatched to retrieve it. With 29-year-old Henry McDonald as coxswain, the boat was 'instantly lowered' and the hat quickly returned to its owner.

Not all distractions were so agreeable. As the *Cospatrick* lay becalmed in the tropics, the measures which in temperate conditions had maintained an acceptable level of hygiene were found wanting. Gastro-intestinal complaints became commonplace, with young children most affected. Diarrhoea and dehydration exacted their toll and eight infants failed to recover, their deaths hastened, in McDonald's judgement, by their mothers' lack of care.

After weeks of slow progress during which no other vessel was sighted, *Cospatrick* was 'spoken' by the ship *Ben Nevis* on 28 October at latitude 11°S, longitude 34°W.[27] This encounter on the Eastern Atlantic seaboard 180 miles from Maceió, Brazil, brought a change of fortune and favourable winds. For the next 20 days the old ship made steady if unspectacular progress on a southeasterly course toward the Cape of Good Hope, achieving, on average, 150 miles each day. On the ninth day of this run Mary Whitehead, wife of Warwickshire butcher Edward Whitehead, gave birth to the couple's first child.

At noon on 17 November independent solar observations by McDonald and 35-year-old First Mate Charles Romaine fixed the vessel's position as latitude 37° 15′ S, longitude 12° 25′ E, some 220 miles to the southwest of the Cape. Once around the southern tip of Africa there was every expectation for a fast passage across the Southern Ocean, under the influence of the strong westerly winds that prevail in the high latitudes. But by nightfall the *Cospatrick* was sailing in light airs and rolling extravagantly in a heavy beam sea. At 9 p.m. James Cadle delivered Mary Fitzgerald, wife of the vessel's schoolmaster, of a still-born child, while emigrants seeking entertainment on the upper deck struggled to keep their footing during an impromptu dance. At 10 p.m. the ship's routines took over, lights below deck were extinguished and, apart from the quiet gamblers in the single men's compartment, the passengers went to their bunks. Later in the night there was so little way on the ship that Quartermaster Thomas Lewis, a 46-year-old Anglesey man, had trouble in holding the vessel to her course. At 11.45 p.m. McDonald, officer in charge of the eight-to-twelve watch, made his final round of the deck before being relieved by Romaine. McDonald found everything to be in order, and shortly after midnight passed management of the ship to his relief. At the same time Lewis handed the helm to Quartermaster Henry Crompton and in a few muttered words informed him of the ship's heading and the difficulty he was having in maintaining steerage way. With the change of watch completed, McDonald went to his cabin below the poop, while the other members of the eight-to-twelve headed for their bunks in the forecastle.

McDonald shared a cabin with Romaine, having given up his own when it became the issuing room for emigrant provisions. His first act on coming off watch was to light up a pipe and have a smoke before turning in. He was barely asleep when, at 12.45 a.m., he heard cries of 'Fire!', the clamour of the warning bell, and the sound of running feet on the deck overhead. Although unclothed, he leapt out into the passageway leading to the saloon, practically colliding with Captain Elmslie, who ordered him forward to find the cause of the alarm. On reaching the forecastle head, McDonald was appalled to see smoke pouring from the fore-scuttle. Charles Romaine was already at work, organising the sailors of his watch as they brought the fire-pumps into action.

The fore-scuttle, the forward-most of *Cospatrick*'s five hatchways, was a vertical wooden shaft, 3 feet by 4 feet, passing through the forecastle and providing access to the boatswain's locker below. The shaft also gave entry to the forepeak, which was beneath the locker and on the same level as the lower hold. The stores in the boatswain's locker were used to maintain the ship's hull and rigging, and many were highly flammable – pitch and Stockholm tar, turpentine, varnish, paraffin, and linseed oil. Moreover, about 30 tons of coal for use in the ship's galley and distillation plant lay in the forepeak. In the hold, which was separated from the forepeak only by a bulkhead of planks, were other combustibles and nearly 6000 gallons of spirits.

It was the nocturnal card-players in the single men's compartment who had first raised the alarm. At the forward end of their quarters was a large ventilation grill that communicated with the fore-scuttle. When smoke began to waft through the grill they rushed to the upper deck in a state of great agitation. Shouting out that fire was in the boatswain's locker, they alerted the watch on deck and woke the seamen in the forecastle.

The sailors manning the fire-hose directed a stream of water down the fore-scuttle, but despite frantic efforts flames erupted from the shaft. McDonald ran aft to report to Elmslie, and advised him to keep the ship before the wind. Better for the flames to be directed forward than give them the chance to sweep the length of the ship. Aware of his lack of clothing, McDonald then hurried below to dress. Before making his way forward again he helped James Cadle and Nurse Bridget Jones dispose of the signal rockets and fog gun ammunition stored in the ship's hospital. As the incendiaries were being collected and put over the side, the 'tween deck spaces were evacuated and the women and children assembled on the poop.

The rate at which the fire progressed took everyone by surprise. Within 15 minutes of the alarm being sounded, *Cospatrick*'s entire forward section was involved; the boatswain's locker was a mass of flame, and the forecastle and the deck above it were well alight. Tongues of flame leapt skywards from the fore-scuttle and the intense heat forced Romaine's seamen to abandon the fixed Downton fire-pump and drove them from the forecastle head. The ventilation grill in the fore-scuttle allowed free passage of air through the forward bulkhead and was, of course, no barrier to the flames. Fuelled by crude pine-wood furniture and the wood shavings used as mattress-filling, fire engulfed the single men's compartment sending smoke and flame gushing from the fore-hatch. The launch and cutter were stowed on skids at either side of the hatch, and both were soon burning and useless. Their destruction reduced the number of *Cospatrick*'s boats from six to four. Romaine's response to the deteriorating situation was to have the foresail above the fore-hatch hauled up, in the hope of preventing the fire from taking hold in the fore-mast rigging.

This was a critical action; it sealed the fate of the vessel and nearly everyone in her. In the absence of the balancing pressure exerted by the big foresail, the force of wind on the after sails caused the *Cospatrick*'s stern to swing to leeward. Elmsie called to Quartermaster Crompton to correct the swing, but with steerage way now lost Crompton could do nothing as the vessel turned bow to wind. As she did so, a mass of smoke and embers blew aft along the entire length of the upper deck and the roar of the blaze carried to those gathered on the poop. The fire was now directed toward them.

Had the remaining boats been put out and used to drag the *Cospatrick* stern-on to the wind the outcome might have been less certain, but Elmslie failed to give the order. The emigrants, however, were galvanised into action. Fully aware of the danger of the situation, they took up fire-buckets, mess tins – every tub or dish that would hold water – and put them to use. Some also manned the small pump used to draw water from the ship's tanks. *Cospatrick*'s bulwarks were so high it proved impossible to fill the fire-buckets other than at the gangways amidships. A sailor stationed with a bucket at each gangway drew up the water, which was then passed forward along a chain of emigrants in any receptacle that came to hand. This was a desperately inefficient and discouraging process, made all the more difficult by the choking smoke which blanketed the deck. The second Downton fire-pump, the portable unit insisted on by the New Zealand despatching officer, was also relatively ineffective. The inlet hose was barely able to reach the surface of the sea and the pump lost suction whenever the vessel rolled.

Driven by the head-wind, the fire continued to burn its way aft, in the process incinerating the elaborate system of tar-coated shrouds and stays supporting the fore-mast. Flame enveloped the deckhouse immediately behind the mast, and the seamen and emigrants fighting the fire were beaten back. *Cospatrick*'s upper deck was made of hardwood planking four inches thick but this also burned readily. The New Zealand despatching officer, giving voice to a prevailing misconception that teak was difficult to burn, was later to say (presumably incredulously): 'Her deck was teak, she was a teak-built ship entirely, and teak is almost like iron in a fire.'[28] When the flames reached a point on the upper deck midway between the fore- and main-hatches, Elmslie called for volunteers to fight the fire from below decks – but he was asking the impossible. Three men made the attempt, but the heat and the dense smoke forced them to retreat. When McDonald asked whether the surviving boats should be prepared and put over the side, Elmslie replied in the negative and requested that efforts to extinguish the fire be redoubled. Much of his attention was now focused on the wife and child at his side. Distracted by the danger to his family and undone by a lack of preparation and resources, the difficulties he faced were now beyond solution.

In 1873 the Board of Trade had issued a bulletin entitled *Suggestions to Masters of Emigrant Ships Respecting Boats and Fires at Sea*. The document

The *Cospatrick* ablaze. (*The Penny Illustrated Paper*, 1875)

The *Cospatrick* ablaze. (*The Graphic*, 1875)

called on masters and officers to pay special attention of to 'the fearful consequences which must result from want of preparation in the event of accident … and especially of fire.' Captains were advised to hold regular fire and boat drills, and to keep all boats 'in good order, clear and ready for immediate use'. It further advised that ships' crews should be divided into three groups, one to man the fire pumps, another to close off portholes and hatches, and the third to provision the boats and prepare them for lowering. It is not known whether Elmslie was aware of the bulletin as, owing to an oversight, it may not have been placed on the *Cospatrick* prior to departure. Even so, the 'suggestions' it contained were no more than measures any prudent master might consider as common sense. For whatever reason, Elmslie failed to adopt them. The boats were not prepared for launching, nor were they provisioned. As the fire took hold, the need to limit the flow of air into the spaces below decks was overlooked, and all three upper deck hatches – fore, main and after (which gave access to the various sections of the emigrants' quarters) – remained open. Elmslie's decisions were naturally influenced by the small size of his crew and the limited capacity of the ship's boats. Since it took several seamen – perhaps as many as a dozen – between 15 and 20 minutes to get a boat off its skids and safely into the water, he was understandably reluctant to commit a large proportion of his skilled manpower to this task. It also seems that he had no confidence in the ability of the emigrants to be helpful, either in fighting the fire or in assisting with the boats. Of course, in the more than two months since the *Cospatrick* had left Gravesend nothing had been done to ensure that they would be. Hampered by a passenger to crew ratio of ten to one, Elmslie adopted the simplest of strategies: the greater the number of seamen at the pumps, the better the chance of successfully extinguishing the fire. Fighting the fire was the obvious imperative, but by failing to ready the boats he risked everything on a single course of action.

The pine-wood partitions dividing the 'tween deck spaces failed to stem the progress of the fire and the amidships and after compartments became involved in turn. When flame burst from the main-hatch entrance to the married couples' quarters, half-suffocated and disheartened men, singly at first and then in a rush, broke off the unequal battle on the upper deck and made their way to the poop. One of the last to abandon the fight was a 17-year-old ordinary seaman named Edward Cotter. The product of a London slum, Cotter was an intelligent young man, although sometimes disingenuous – as will be seen later. His general appearance – medium height, grey eyes, sallow complexion and light brown hair – is known, thanks to a well-documented brush with the New Zealand judiciary just eight months earlier.[29] As the blaze advanced along *Cospatrick*'s upper deck he persisted for a time with the second fire-pump, but found only Able Seaman Charles Hancock willing to help: 'we two could do no good, two men on a big pump and so we went away'.[30] Cotter then assisted other sailors in drawing water at the gangways but this was also a futile exercise. Eventually he too made his way aft in a fruitless search for a life jacket or lifebuoy.

Recognising what the outcome was likely to be, some gave up quietly and without complaint. Chief Steward Thomas Wakefield, in poor health since the beginning of the voyage and reluctant to face death by drowning, simply went to his cabin beneath the poop and waited to be asphyxiated. He was never seen again. Mary Fitzgerald had stayed below after giving birth, and with her husband and four children perished in the 'tween deck. James Cadle remained true to the best tenets of his profession. He had patients brought up to the poop from the hospital – one a man with a broken leg – and dispensed water to the women and children who were becoming increasingly distressed. 'The screams of the women were awful,' McDonald said later, 'they hung about me, begging me to save them, but a man could not do everything.'[31] The entire after section of the ship and the surrounding sea were now lit up by the flames devouring the upper deck, masts and yards. Fragments of burning canvas and rigging rained down, adding to the chaos.

As panic seized *Cospatrick*'s emigrants, a rush was made for the starboard lifeboat. There was no attempt to assign places according to the 'Women and children first' principle, nor was there any order or control. People literally poured into the boat, totally overwhelming its capacity. Surprisingly, it was mostly women who managed to clamber in, but only because they were the ones closest to hand. As it was about to be lowered – so overloaded that people were hanging from its sides – the iron davits bent under the enormous weight and the stern dipped into the sea. The boat immediately filled and capsized, throwing most of its 80 or so occupants into the water. Those on *Cospatrick*'s poop with their wits still about them tossed in chicken coops, lifebuoys and anything else that would float, but nearly everyone in the boat drowned alongside. Several of the women were initially supported by air trapped in their petticoats and these garments, according to Edward Cotter's dispassionate description, 'served the purpose very well until soaked.'[32] Quartermaster Crompton jumped overboard in an effort to secure the capsized craft, but was dragged under while swimming through the mass of people struggling in the water.

Disregarding Elmslie's instructions, McDonald and Romaine, with Boatswain William Symons and Third Mate Brasher Jones, made an attempt to turn the heavy longboat over and ready it for launching. Symons, six years with Elmslie as *Cospatrick*'s boatswain, was the designated coxswain of the starboard lifeboat, but appears not to have been in it when the davits collapsed. The longboat the four were trying to get upright was stowed keel-up on *Cospatrick*'s port side, close to the after-hatch, with the bow raised on a skid and the stern resting on the poop. Unable to muster the necessary assistance, the men abandoned the task when the boat's bow planking and stem caught alight. A group of seamen and passengers similarly engaged on the starboard side bodily hoisted the smaller captain's gig onto the bulwarks and pushed it into the sea. In the excitement, no one had thought to make the painter fast before putting the boat over and, swamped and empty, it drifted away. With the longboat, gig, and starboard lifeboat now also destroyed or unserviceable, only the port lifeboat remained. With the capacity to save just 30 people, it soon came under siege.

The craft would have shared the fate of its starboard counterpart had it not been for a group of seamen, who, under strict instructions from *Cospatrick*'s officers, admitted other sailors into the boat but vigorously defended it against male passengers. The emigrants took desperate measures, but a wire ridge-line extending around poop at midriff level prevented a wholesale rush. Anyone charging toward the boat had to slow in order to duck beneath the wire, and this gave the sailors the opportunity to beat them back. Knives were undoubtedly drawn, if not used, for it was as natural for a seaman to carry a knife as it was for him to wear trousers. Cotter, who had taken his place in the defensive line, later described how a young Jersey emigrant with a one-gallon can of water strapped to his body attempted to trade the water for a place in the boat, but was turned away. Another man pushed his wife to one side before begging Ordinary Seaman William Wood to admit him, but he too was excluded. However, compassion was not entirely absent and the seamen found places for Edward and Mary Whitehead and their baby born 11 days earlier. Of the dozens of women and children massed on the poop, as many as 10 may have been allowed into the boat, while a few male emigrants, who had entered before the seamen took control, retained their places in the ensuing confusion.

As the lifeboat was being defended, *Cospatrick*'s fore-mast, its supporting rigging burnt through, crashed into the sea in a torrent of sparks and debris. Flames poured from the after-hatch. Elmslie, recognising that time was now very short, gave his final command: '*Let every man look after himself!*' Immediately, a mass of frantic emigrants surged toward the lifeboat, threatening to overwhelm it. No order to lower away was given, but a seaman stationed in the boat amidships cast off the lowering pendants of Clifford's 'Patent Boat Lowering Gear' and the small craft descended rapidly toward the sea. Left on the poop were more than 350 people – many of whom would have prevented the boat from leaving had it been equipped with conventional lowering tackle. It was then that 'the most terrible of cries were raised, for the little boat was literally crammed and those who were left in the ship saw that there was no hope'.[33] McDonald spent his last moments on the *Cospatrick* in an unsuccessful attempt to find a boat's compass, and escaped only by going hand over hand down the falls after the boat had reached the water. A number of emigrants, spurred on by the example, either threw themselves into the boat or also entered by way of the falls – one woman managing to strip the flesh from her palms as she slid down the rope. Charles Romaine and a young Irish woman named Mary Shea swam to the boat after jumping from the poop and were hauled on board.

Although McDonald was the lifeboat's designated coxswain, Romaine, as the senior officer, assumed command. Fearing that the heavily laden craft would be capsized by people in the water, he kept well clear of the ship and beyond the area of sea illuminated by the flames. While the boat's occupants watched in horrified silence, *Cospatrick*'s main-mast crashed onto the poop, killing many who had sought its shelter. As the heat of the blaze intensified, this last refuge became totally uninhabitable. Stay and burn, or jump into the sea? There was no choice. Parents flung their children overboard and then leapt after them. William Wray, a 38-year-old emigrant from County Down, was seen to throw his wife Mary and several of their nine children over the side, before jumping himself. Dozens of others did likewise. True to the traditions of the merchant service, Alexander Emslie remained at his post to the last. He had made no effort to secure a place in the boat for Henrietta, and she stayed at his side throughout. At the end they jumped into the sea together. James Cadle gathered their four-year-old son in his arms before following them into the water.

Most of the emigrants were non-swimmers who drowned almost immediately, but some succeeded in clutching floating spars and by so doing managed to extend their lives by a few more hours. Thirty minutes after the port lifeboat had got away the fire reached the after section of the lower hold, where 40 tons of spirits were stowed. The alcohol ignited explosively – a cloud of flaming vapour burst over the poop, the mizzen-mast went by the board and the stern blew out. It was just 3 a.m. Charles Romaine's twelve-to-four watch, a period fittingly known as the graveyard watch, was still one hour short of completion; *Cospatrick*'s transformation from a well-found ship carrying nearly 500 men, women, and children to a blazing wreck devoid of life had taken place in a little over two hours.

Cospatrick's port lifeboat – the only boat to be launched successfully on the night of 17 November 1874 – pictured in 1873, before being fitted with Clifford's 'Patent Boat Lowering Gear'. (Enhanced detail from the De Maus photograph on page 23.)

5. HENRY MCDONALD'S LIFEBOAT

Strong gale, with a heavy sea running. Five deaths.
Cut a couple for the blood and flesh.

Entry in the diary of Henry McDonald for Monday 23 November 1874.[1]

The port lifeboat stayed close to the blazing hulk for the rest of the night. Exhausted by their efforts to subdue the fire and numbed by the extent of the disaster, the boat's occupants were nevertheless hopeful of an early rescue. *Cospatrick* had become a beacon that any passing ship would turn from its course to investigate, and even after dawn the pall of smoke hanging over the wreck continued to signal her distress. Thirty-five people were crammed into the lifeboat's 24½-feet length. Although only five more than the boat's estimated capacity, it was a load that reduced the freeboard to just six inches. *Cospatrick*'s seamen figured prominently among the survivors – 14 of the 44 crew members were present, including the two ship's officers, Romaine and McDonald. Thomas Lewis, Edward Cotter, and Charlie Hancock had all gained places, having fought for them against the flood of emigrants. Lewis had been in the starboard lifeboat during the disastrous attempt to get it away and, using the fore-tackle, had hauled himself back onto the poop when the davits collapsed – a feat allowed by upper body strength developed over half a lifetime of working aloft at sea. Cotter had at first held back when told by McDonald to take his place in the boat; protesting that his assigned position was in the launch burnt earlier, he expected that preference would be given to saving the women and children. Able seamen Thomas Doughery, Charlie Cunningham, Frank Bellifanti, John Langdon, Harry Boscobie, Alfred Nicolle, and Thomas Turvey were in the boat, as were Ordinary Seaman William Wood and the ship's butcher, Alfred Dutton. Dutton had placed half a sheep's carcass in the boat, but this was soon thrown over the side to make room for one more person. In addition to Mary Shea and the Whitehead family, emigrants known to have found places in the boat were John and Caroline Marsh from Warwickshire; Bartholomew and Catherine Geary from Cork; Catherine Harvey aged 18 and her older brother William from Belfast; Arthur Colley, one of the ship's constables appointed by Cadle; Thomas Bentley, a 37-year-old labourer from Lancashire; 18-year-old James Mahar, a son of Thomas and Mary Mahar; David Lewis aged 11, youngest of son of Montgomeryshire cowman Thomas Lewis (as distinct from *Cospatrick*'s quartermaster of the same name); and one of the nine Wray children – a boy. Also in the boat were six other emigrants, three or four of whom were women, whose names are not known. Shortly after dawn the boat's occupants spotted Robert Byron, a 34-year-old navvy from Ayr, who was clutching a floating spar. Risking the capsize of their deeply laden craft, they pulled him on board.

Except for one gallon of water there were no provisions in the boat and much of its basic equipment was missing. It had a rudder and mast, but no sail and just three intact oars. One oar had been broken in two as the boat was being launched, and a fifth, normally carried as a spare, could not be found. Nor was there a baler or a water-cask. Many items had been removed a few days earlier, when the boat was being prepared for painting and had not been replaced. This extraordinary oversight later resulted in questions being asked about the competence of *Cospatrick*'s master and officers. The lack of a baler – a serious and immediate concern as the boat was taking in water through strained hull planking – was providentially overcome when a few tins from the emigrants' quarters were found floating nearby. With the bottom cut out and the neck plugged with rags, a tin made an adequate substitute.

Toward noon the starboard lifeboat, now right way up and containing 26 men and boys, came into view. Its salvage owed much to the efforts of 19-year-old Able Seaman John (Scottie) McNeill, who, along with a number of other sailors and emigrants, had spent much of the night clinging to floating wreckage. Seeing the capsized craft near to them at dawn, McNeill secured enough co-operation from those around him to get it upright and baled out. For men chilled to the bone after spending several hours partially immersed in cold seawater – the surface-water temperature at the site of *Cospatrick*'s abandonment is usually around 57 degrees Fahrenheit (14 degrees Celsius) in November – it was a notable feat, with the boat being righted only after six energy-sapping attempts.[2] Post-Second World War research suggests likely survival times of six to nine hours for normally clad, healthy adults immersed in water at 57 degrees Fahrenheit, while children, with a higher surface area to body mass ratio, cool more quickly and experience the onset of hypothermia earlier than adults.[3] Even so, three boys from the *Cospatrick* managed to survive their night in the water and now found themselves included in the starboard lifeboat's complement. Astonishingly – the more so because many of the survivors were stark naked – the boat had been emptied of water using men's caps, somehow retained by the owners during their plunge into the sea. Lacking every item of gear normally carried – even a rudder – the boat was paddled along using ripped-up bottom boards.

As the two craft drew together the demoralised occupants of the starboard lifeboat called out that they needed an officer. Following a brief discussion with Romaine (ended by his emphatic instruction: '*You go!*') McDonald agreed to transfer; but, to make the numbers in the boats more nearly equal, took with him the emigrant Thomas Bentley and seamen Thomas Lewis and Edward Cotter. All three men transferred voluntarily, although young Cotter had second thoughts. As he was about to step across the gap between the two boats he hesitated and looked back to where Kate Harvey was seated next to Charles Romaine. It was the last he was to see of her – 'a bright Irish girl' who had taken his fancy – and the scene remained etched on his memory for the rest of his life. Bentley's willingness to make the switch came from the fact that he would be reunited with his 11-year-old son, Frederick, one of the three boys in the boat; however, two other sons and his wife and daughter were missing. Lewis, a man of few words but vastly experienced in small boat handling, may well have felt that, with its somewhat lesser load, the starboard lifeboat had the better chance of staying afloat. McDonald too was not entirely dissatisfied with the change. He believed that the women in the port lifeboat constituted an added danger; being more likely to panic than men (in his opinion), they might cause it to capsize if the weather worsened. Even after the readjustment in personnel, both boats were considerably overloaded – the port lifeboat now contained 32 people, while its starboard counterpart held 30. McDonald's own assessment of their capabilities was that properly equipped and with just 20 occupants, each would have been 'comfortable in all weathers'.[4]

In exchange for his co-operation, Romaine gave McDonald one of the improvised balers, together with one good oar and the blade from the broken one; Mary Shea unselfishly passed over her petticoat for use as a sail. As his first task in the starboard lifeboat, McDonald organised a redistribution of clothing to provide for those having little or none. Several of the better-clad emigrants were pressured into donating garments to less-well-off neighbours, while Cotter gave one of his two shirts to Scottie McNeill, who otherwise had nothing at all; Lewis's dungaree over-trousers and McDonald's waistcoat and cap were also given to others. In addition to McNeill, the other crew members in the boat from the time it was righted were Able Seaman Robert Hamilton, a black man from Port Maria, Jamaica; Peter Cope, the ship's baker; and William King, the emigrants' cook. A rudimentary mast was fashioned from the craft's bottom boards and to it the seamen attached Mary Shea's petticoat sail.[5] The intact oar, held in a loop of rope at the boat's sternpost, became a replacement for the missing rudder.

The two lifeboats stayed close to the still-burning remains of the *Cospatrick* – although not too close. People supported by spars floating near to the vessel could be heard calling for help, but were not approached simply because there was no room for them to be taken in. Those in the boats knew that each additional occupant would further reduce what was already a minute margin of safety, and with hardened resolve they kept clear. By doing so they passed up the opportunity to collect cordage and sail canvas from the spars; if used to rig the boats for sail, these materials would have greatly improved their seaworthiness.

On the afternoon of 19 November, 40 hours after the outbreak of the fire, *Cospatrick*'s charred and smouldering hulk finally sank; burnt down to the water line over its entire length, the wreck was dragged to the bottom by the weight of railway iron in the hold. As the glowing timbers were quenched and the last plume of smoke and steam dispersed, all hope that a passing vessel would be attracted to the scene also disappeared. There was now no point in lingering: Romaine and McDonald decided that their best chance lay in keeping the boats together and heading for the Cape of Good Hope, which they knew to be about 250 miles to the northeast. However, the total absence of navigational aids – they were without chart, sextant, chronometer or compass – meant that the journey would be attempted while steering by the sun and the stars, with no possibility of determining an exact position. Nor could any allowance be made for the effect of the Benguela Current, which, sweeping up from its origins in the deep waters of the Antarctic, would tend to drive the boats northward along Southern Africa's western coast. Considering the state of the two craft and the people they held, it was an ambitious undertaking, but the closer the boats could get to the Cape, the better would be the odds of encountering a vessel heading into or out of Cape Town. The decision to make for land was welcomed by the survivors, who were surprisingly 'light-hearted and cheerful rather than otherwise'; there was a general feeling that they would soon be at the Cape with a glass of wine in hand.[6] Having emerged from one catastrophe, most gave no thought to the possibility that a more dreadful one might soon overtake them.

But for the next two days a biting wind blew from the south. Sleep was impossible during the bitterly cold nights and, drenched by sea-spray, all that the boats' occupants could do was huddle together and wait for the relative warmth of day. Not surprisingly, the physical condition of the more poorly clothed deteriorated rapidly and morale plummeted. There was no further talk of the delights of the Cape; everyone was now obsessed with the lack of fresh water.

Without replenishment, the water content of the human body falls steadily, owing to the processes of excretion and transpiration, and water loss leads to a battery of neurological problems. Dehydration corresponding to a five per cent decrease in body weight is associated with headaches, irritability and feelings of light-headedness, while a decrease of eight to ten per cent impairs one's ability to perform simple tasks; further losses lead to hallucinations and delirium. Dehydration amounting to a decrease of 15 to 20 per cent of body weight is often fatal, and in a marine environment this condition is usually reached after six or seven days.[7] On 21 November *Cospatrick*'s survivors had been without fresh water for four days. Driven by thirst and without regard for the consequences, some began to drink from the sea.

That evening the wind force increased, causing the overloaded boats to labour heavily. Soon both needed constant bailing. At 9 p.m. McDonald caught a glimpse of Romaine's craft as its crew fought to keep it afloat, but at dawn his boat was alone on the windswept sea. Romaine's luck had finally run out; he had survived the abandonment of sinking vessels on two previous occasions – the first in 1866, after the *Cossipore* stranded off Sagar Island near Calcutta, and the second, five years later, when the *Challenger* foundered in the Atlantic.[8] The wreck of the *Cospatrick* was far less forgiving, and for Charles Romaine there was no third tale of survival. His boat was most probably swamped during the night of 21 November 1874 and, along with everyone on board, was never seen or heard of again.

For the next 24 hours the sea continued to run high. McDonald, who throughout the ordeal 'kept a little bit of a diary' recorded how Thomas Bentley at the steering oar missed his stroke as the boat slid down the face of a wave, and while unbalanced fell over the side[9]. A good swimmer (a rarity among landsmen of the time), Bentley could be heard calling for assistance as the boat continued its down-wind run, but there was no stopping to pick him up, lest the boat broach-to in the attempt. He was the first of four to die on 22 November. The others, less strong-willed than their companions, had consumed large amounts of salt water during the preceding 24 hours. They became deranged and incoherent, frequently attempting to jump over the side before falling into a fatal lethargy. One of the unfortunates was Edward Bickersteth, the only fare-paying passenger known to have found a place in the boats. Bickersteth, an engineer from Birkenhead, had been in the boat at the time of its attempted launching and, despite being 'fearfully bruised' in the resulting capsize, regained his place after it was salvaged by Scottie McNeill. 'Half-drowned' by his efforts, McNeill never recovered and was so incapacitated that he was unable to help with the boat's management.[10] He too was among the first to die. Along with those of the others, his body was put over the side after first being stripped of its clothing.

Throughout the next day the depopulation of McDonald's lifeboat continued. More survivors had become deranged after drinking seawater, with one believing that he could see a distant sandy beach with a white house standing on it, and imploring for the boat to be steered in that direction. The hallucination was almost convincing to Cotter, who, though ravenously hungry and at the edge of reality, was surprisingly unaffected by thirst.[11] Of the five who died on 23 November, most did so in their sleep. 'The biggest, fattest and healthiest-looking men went off first,' Cotter said afterwards.[12] They would crowd together in an immobile group and later, when the mass of bodies moved again, there were one or two who could not be roused.

The spectre of cannibalism, which had increasingly dominated the thoughts of the boat's occupants in the preceding days, now found full expression. Two of the bodies were cut open – probably by the quartermaster, Thomas Lewis, although this point was never fully established – and the livers were sliced into portions and served out.[13] The scene was one of great barbarism, in which the participants found they 'had to almost fight with a savage maniac for a share of what was necessary to keep … alive.'[14] In Lewis's grim words it was a time when 'a man would eat anything'. The flesh of each corpse was deeply incised and, in grisly communion, the survivors pressed their lips to the wounds and sucked the blood and tissue fluid from them. The spectacle – the living numbered 21 at this stage – was reminiscent of scavengers clustered around carrion.

Despite the limitations of his craft's dilapidated rig, McDonald persisted in trying to reach the Cape. Although unable to judge the boat's position, he was aware that the sea-temperature was increasing daily and guessed that they were making progress to the north. He could not tell that none was being made toward the east. He had organised the seamen into watches, with Cotter, Lewis and Hamilton each taking turn about. During Hamilton's watch the only oar was lost when he fell asleep while steering, necessitating another being cobbled together from the boat's remaining bottom boards. As the day progressed the weather deteriorated and by nightfall a full gale was blowing and the seas were heavy. The seamen tore out the boat's seats and stern sheets to make a drogue which, when streamed from the bow, helped the boat lie more easily; fastened only by strands of rope unravelled from the painter (the intact painter not being long enough for the purpose), the drogue was lost when they parted. Thomas Lewis was now fully in his element. The boat-handling skills acquired as a boy off the rugged Anglesey coast had from the outset made him the most valuable person in the boat; illiterate and unassuming, he nevertheless possessed the strength and expertise to keep the small craft afloat in the teeth of a South Atlantic storm. McDonald was later to describe him as 'my right hand' and during the worst moments of the night it was Lewis to whom he turned. Another drogue was improvised and attached to the boat by a rope made from the braces, belts and clothing of the dead. Hove to, the craft lived through the gale despite broaching-to and half-filling when this second makeshift rope also failed.

With most of its interior fittings cannibalised for use in the drogues, McDonald's lifeboat was little more than a shell. It rode higher and more safely for being relieved of the weight of the dead, but was to ride higher still as the wastage of its occupants continued. Six more died on 24 November, and the bodies were again utilised by the survivors before being thrown overboard. Cotter took every opportunity to obtain nourishment but his condition had fallen away during the preceding 24 hours and he was near to giving up. He was sustained by Lewis, who, though surrounded by blood, madness and death, remained optimistic of his own chances and encouraged the younger man. He kept Cotter occupied in steering and baling, and prevented him from falling into the deep sleep which had so often signalled the end.

It was hot during the following day, with light breezes blowing from the south. 'We all felt very bad,' recorded McDonald, whose pencilled diary entries had deteriorated to a barely legible scrawl. His fingers were so swollen that he could barely hold the pencil and it was the last occasion he was able to write. The storms had passed over the boat without favouring the occupants with rain, and it was now their eighth day without fresh water. Death claimed seven more and the survivors were reduced to eight, three of whom were deranged. Apart from the sea around them there was only one source of liquid, and both the sane and the crazed lacerated the flesh of their dead companions and sucked at the cuts.

Shortly before dawn on the ninth day a big, grey-painted barque slid noiselessly past them. Running before the wind and no more than 50 yards distant, she passed close enough to leave the boat rocking in her wake. The vessel's appearance was so unexpected that some of the boat's occupants believed her to be an apparition. Lewis called out and thought he heard an answering hail, but the barque failed to turn back. The mood of despondency that settled over the boat after this unproductive encounter was not shared by Lewis. Realising that they must have found their way into a shipping lane, he knew that where there was one ship there were likely to be others. But soon after the chance meeting with the barque, one of the madmen succumbed, leaving just seven people still alive. Of the seven, four were seamen – McDonald, Lewis, Cotter, and Hamilton – while three were male emigrants. Jeremiah Leuchan, a 24-year-old agricultural labourer from Cork, was one of the three, but the other two are less readily identifiable. They were probably John McBride, a 27-year-old farm labourer from Devonshire, and Frederick Bentley, the 11-year-old son of Thomas Bentley, who, four days earlier, had watched as his father drowned.[15] However, both died during the night of the twenty-sixth leaving Jeremiah Leuchan as the last of *Cospatrick*'s 433 passengers still alive.

Leuchan was the youngest son of an Irish farmer. As was customary, the father had willed the family land to the oldest of his male offspring, leaving Jeremiah with an uncertain future if he chose to remain in Ireland. His decision to emigrate was taken only after a promise of financial assistance from his elder brother. But on the morning of 27 November 1874 he was beyond regretting his choice. Having drunk large quantities of salt water during the night and under the delusion that he was about to be conscripted into the army, on three occasions he tried to avoid this imaginary fate by jumping into the sea. Cotter, now physically more able than his companions, helped hold him back and while doing so spied a mass of drifting kelp, which he hauled on board. When crushed, the float bladders and the small crabs living among its fronds yielded a brackish liquid that came as a godsend to the boat's occupants. It was their first stroke of good fortune in ten days, although by this time all had drunk seawater. One of the dead from the previous night was put over the side, but the seamen lacked the strength to deal with the other and it was apparent that the end was near. McDonald, who had coolly measured his own decline against that of his companions, felt that he might last another 12 hours – but not longer. Squalls all around the boat offered the prospect of rain, but never came close enough to fulfil the promise. By afternoon Hamilton was comatose and Lewis nearly so. McDonald had been sleeping but awoke to find Leuchan gnawing at the heel of his boot. As he feebly kicked the madman, away he looked up to see a full-rigged vessel emerging from a rain shower to leeward. Sails slatting, the stranger turned into the wind and hove to. The lifeboat drifted slowly down to her.

6. COSPATRICK'S SECOND MATE

The second mate's is proverbially a dog's berth. He is neither officer nor man …
He is one to whom little is given and of whom much is required.

Two Years Before the Mast, Richard Henry Dana, 1840.

The vessel that happened upon McDonald's lifeboat on the afternoon of 27 November 1874 was the 1436-ton Liverpool-registered sailing ship *British Sceptre*. Commanded by Captain William Jahnke, and bound for Dundee from Calcutta with a cargo of jute, *British Sceptre* had rounded the Cape of Good Hope two days earlier. Her subsequent northward progress was marked by periodic encounters with floating debris and, as this could only have come from a recent shipwreck, Jahnke ordered his men to keep a sharp lookout for possible survivors.

At first the boat seemed just another piece of battered wreckage. As the largest surviving fragment from the *Cospatrick*, it had been driven the farthest by wind and current and lay at the end of the trail marking her destruction. It was a trail that terminated at latitude 28° 50′ S, longitude 12° 44′ E – a position more than 500 miles to the north of the vessel's abandonment. Hovering above the boat were large numbers of boobies – gannet-like birds known to follow any craft carrying the sick, the dying or the dead. Although Jahnke's telescope revealed no other sign of life he changed course toward the derelict, only to lose sight of it when *British Sceptre* became caught up in a passing squall. When the boat next came into view his signals failed to draw a response, and it was not until *British Sceptre* had closed to within a few yards that he could see it held several persons. All appeared helpless and exhausted.

As Jahnke manoeuvred to bring his vessel alongside, the state of the boat's occupants became more clearly apparent. There were six in all, but of these one was dead and the others barely alive. It was obvious that the flesh of the corpse had been used to sustain the living. Jeremiah Leuchan presented as a horrifying spectacle, being 'stripped naked up to his waist, his feet swollen, full of sores, himself raving mad'. One of *British Sceptre*'s seamen was lowered into the boat at the end of a rope to find all the living in appalling condition: 'their starved-looking faces and emaciated bodies … but too plainly revealed the dreadful sufferings which had been endured.'[1] McDonald tried to communicate with his rescuers, but could only croak out a few words after first wetting his mouth with salt water. He and the others were so weakened by their ordeal they had to be laid in blankets before being hoisted on board. They were immediately taken to the comfort of the ship's saloon.

As there was no doctor on *British Sceptre*, the task of nursing the survivors fell to Jahnke himself. It was fortunate that a long period of fair weather followed the rescue, as this released him from many of the normal demands of captaincy and gave time for the attempt. His commonsense treatment called for water, dilute brandy, nourishing food, and warm baths, but the prescription came far too late for Jeremiah Leuchan. The physiological damage caused by the high salt concentrations in his tissues proved irreversible and he died within 24 hours of being rescued. Toward the end he had a brief moment of sanity, recognising Lewis, who was lying beside him, and dying with a smile on his lips. Despite being rescued, Hamilton felt certain that he would not survive. He told the others of his premonition, which proved to be correct as he died on 2 December and, like Leuchan, was buried at sea.

McDonald, Lewis, and Cotter clung to life. After receiving their first food, they 'manifested a very ravenous desire and would have eaten enormously if they could have got it.'[2] Cotter was quartered in *British Sceptre*'s small deckhouse, and on feeling the need for water would crawl out to help himself from a cask on deck. His thirst lasted just three days, but hunger was a different matter: 'There was no limit to it,' he said later. 'I was really ashamed of the way I took food.'[3] After initially making progress toward recovery, McDonald's condition worsened. He became severely affected by diarrhoea, almost certainly brought on by over-eating, and this took him 'almost down to death's-door.' Jahnke, acknowledging

The survivors sight the *British Sceptre*. *(The Graphic, 1875)*

his limited medical skills and concerned for all three men, determined on a course for nearby St Helena. They were landed at Jamestown on 6 December, nine days after being picked up. McDonald and Jahnke had developed a close bond, and at the moment of parting exchanged stilted letters expressing feelings of mutual regard. McDonald thanked *British Sceptre*'s crew for their 'vigilance and promptness at that critical moment', and recorded that the survivors would 'ever cherish a grateful remembrance of [their] kindness and attention.'[4] They were particularly fortunate, not least because ships' captains did not always stop to examine apparently derelict boats. But Jahnke's actions were consistent with a belief that it was no more than his duty to rescue the distressed men from the 'frightful and painful circumstances' in which they found themselves.[5]

Lewis and McDonald were sent to the local hospital, but Cotter was thought sufficiently recovered to be lodged in a boarding house. This accommodation turned out to be vermin infested and he complained until he was reunited with his shipmates. *British Sceptre*'s crew had raised £8 12s to aid the men and a collection taken up at St Helena contributed a further £18. Much of Cotter's share would be spent on food.

When the saga of *Cospatrick*'s voyage was laid before the St Helena authorities, the scale of the catastrophe was immediately apparent. Only two boats, containing just 62 people out of the 479 on board, had got clear of the vessel; and of the 30 emigrants and crew in McDonald's lifeboat only he, Lewis, and Cotter were alive to tell the tale. Although the fate of Romaine's craft was not known at this time, both Jahnke and McDonald felt that it could not have survived. McDonald was sure that it had been lost three days after the *Cospatrick* was abandoned, while Jahnke was equally certain that had the boat still been afloat *British Sceptre* would have happened upon it during her passage north from the Cape. After interviewing the survivors, St Helena's Governor, Hudson Janisch, soberly concluded that 'the details [of the disaster] are exceedingly distressing, and will give the wreck a place among the worst of the melancholy accounts already recorded.'[6] And so it proved, but it was a further three weeks before news of the tragedy reached Britain.

On 9 December the survivors, together with Janisch's official report,[7] left for Plymouth on the fast mail-steamer *Nyanza*. Cotter travelled as a second-class passenger and throughout the voyage remained obsessed with food. A bribe to the pantryman ensured that he received double helpings at meal times, and it was to be several months before this abnormal appetite subsided. On Christmas Day – a Friday – *Nyanza* called briefly at Madeira, where summary accounts of the disaster were cabled to Lloyd's and *Cospatrick*'s owners. The telegram to Shaw Savill reached their London office at 10 p.m. on the same day, but owing to the festive celebrations of the weekend remained unopened until the following Monday. The delay meant that the first sketchy reports of *Cospatrick*'s loss did not appear in the London newspapers until Tuesday 29 December.[8] They were greeted with confusion and disbelief, and the magnitude of the disaster was at first not comprehended. Because one published account incorrectly stated

The Cape Mail Steamer *Nyanza*.

that *Cospatrick* had sunk close to Tristan da Cunha, hopes were raised that Charles Romaine's lifeboat might have landed safely in that remote group of islands. This mood of optimism quickly disappeared when it became clear that the actual position of the sinking was some 1100 miles to the east.[9]

Included among the 429 emigrants to have lost their lives on the *Cospatrick* were 247 from England, 109 Irish, 42 Scots, 13 Welsh, and 10 Channel Islanders.[10] Virtually every county in England was represented in the passenger list, but the effects of the tragedy encompassed the whole of Britain. Because a high proportion of the emigrants were country people, rural villages were deeply affected. No fewer than 17 members of the intertwined Townsend and Hedges families of Shipton-under-Wychwood were among the dead. New Mains in Larnarkshire had 10 villagers on the ill-fated ship. Among them were a young couple, Maggie McQueen and John Torrance, who had intended to marry as soon as they reached Auckland, and three brothers – Robert, John, and William Livingstone – the only surviving male members of an orphaned family. John Anderson, a 28-year-old New Mains villager, had been in McDonald's lifeboat from the first and in death had sustained the survivors. The disaster cast a long shadow over this community, 'striking the tiny hamlet with double force its tale of woe … at every corner little groups may be seen discussing the appalling calamity, and condoling with friends and relatives of those … deprived of life'.[11] Scenes such as those in New Mains were repeated in villages across the land.

Since only seamen had survived, suspicions were voiced that their safety had been secured at the expense of the passengers in their charge. A telegram from the British Consul in Madeira to New Zealand's Agent-General in London, received on 29 December, revealed further details of the catastrophe, including the fact that the survivors had resorted to cannibalism – 'the most horrible expedient of shipwrecked men.'[12] As the telegram also made known that McDonald, Lewis, and Cotter had taken passage on the *Nyanza*, which was daily expected at Plymouth, interest and speculation mounted. Hungry for first-hand information, a huge press contingent converged on the southern seaport to await the steamer's arrival.

Among the more astute representatives of the press was Archibald Forbes, a special correspondent to the London newspaper *The Daily News*. Forbes, a veteran who had covered famine in India and the Franco-Prussian war of 1870, knew how to get his story. He had arranged for news of *Nyanza*'s entry into the English Channel to be telegraphed from Lizard Point, and had the tug *Volunteer* awaiting orders at Plymouth Docks. The expected telegram arrived at his hotel at 6 p.m. on 31 December and despite a full gale blowing in the Channel he immediately proceeded into Plymouth Sound on *Volunteer*. A wild sea was running, compelling the tug to shelter behind a wave-swept breakwater and deterring less hardy newsmen from similar attempts. At 8 p.m. *Nyanza*'s navigation lights came into view, and even before pratique had been obtained from port authorities, *Volunteer* deposited Forbes on board. He quickly sought out *Cospatrick*'s survivors, and struck a deal for their exclusive stories.[13]

Forbes was at first disconcerted on meeting McDonald, whom he found to be secretive and taciturn, although 'possessed of a considerable degree of intelligence'. He summed up the second mate as 'a canny Scot' if not 'a black Celt', and 'of a type not to believe in the existence of [his] own grandmother.'[14] Initially reluctant to talk, McDonald was encouraged to do so only after Forbes passed himself off as a fellow Scot, and one familiar with McDonald's home town of Montrose. For his part,

Henry McDonald (top), Edward Cotter (left) and Thomas Lewis. (*The Graphic*, 1875)

McDonald was having difficulty with coping and had not slept well since being plucked from the lifeboat. As his story spilled out it was embellished by occasional comments from Lewis and Cotter, but all three men tried to minimise the part that cannibalism had played in their survival. Throughout the interview, *Volunteer*'s captain, still under instruction from Forbes, kept his tug alongside *Nyanza* to prevent her being boarded from other vessels. Outraged newsmen on the government steamer *Sir Francis Drake* were forced to lie off while their rival secured his scoop from the comfort of *Nyanza*'s chief steward's cabin. When the correspondents eventually managed to board, they found McDonald close-mouthed and Lewis and Cotter similarly uncommunicative. According to McDonald, this was because Shaw, Savill & Co. had instructed them not to talk to reporters, a claim that the company later emphatically denied. The newsmen were able to glean some information, but only from pages of the *St Helena Guardian*, which had published McDonald's narrative account of the disaster shortly after *British Sceptre*'s arrival in Jamestown. *Nyanza*'s enterprising sailors made copies of the *Guardian* available at up to £15 apiece.

A keen interest was shown in the survivors' physical appearance. *Nyanza*'s passengers had found difficulty in understanding how men who had been through so much could look so well, and the correspondents were similarly intrigued. Cotter was variously seen to be 'plump and full-faced', or 'hearty and fresh-looking', despite having nearly died of thirst and lack of nourishment just four weeks earlier.[15] Lewis and McDonald, deeply tanned and weather-beaten, also appeared to be in good physical health. Lewis's recovery had been slower than that of the others, and he seemed much older than his 46 years. He himself felt that his recent experiences had added ten years to his age. Forbes had penetrated the Welshman's gruff exterior only with difficulty, but on doing so discovered the 'wonderful energy and self-reliance of Lewis, whose courage had never given way [and which] carried him through everything.'[16]

The men were mobbed on being put ashore, and subjected to 'pushing, crushing and rushing … as unseemly as it was happily uncommon.' Furious at being denied access to a major story, the reporters came close to blows in their efforts to obtain interviews. This behaviour, and the fact that Forbes had almost certainly used bribery to secure McDonald's compliance, was almost unheard of among the responsible English press of the time. Comparisons were drawn with unscrupulous American methods,[17] and Forbes was seen to have acted with a 'Yankee smartness and selfishness' which failed to allow the 'full and true particulars of the disaster' to be disclosed.[18] As much as anything else, the 'full and true particulars' concerned the disclosures of cannibalism in McDonald's lifeboat. At one point the survivors appeared to lower their guard when they spoke of an occasion when Lewis, to save Cotter's life, had encouraged him to eat the liver of one of the dead. Cotter refused to do so 'unless his officer did', but eventually all three had 'a small portion'. Lewis said that the unnatural food had no flavour, while Cotter, perhaps tongue in cheek, described the taste as 'just like cream milk'.[19] These delicate comments were received with scepticism, and among some in the press it was assumed they were made to mask actions even more unspeakable.[20] Under intense questioning Cotter incautiously admitted to drinking 'whenever a vein was opened.' Although not elaborated on at the time, the statement does suggest that some of the lifeboat's occupants may have been bled to death. Cotter was quick to blame McDonald for his reticence: 'I'll tell you all you like only the [2nd] mate won't let me. I asked him and he won't. It ain't my fault.' He denied having been bribed, claiming to have declined an offer of £100.[21] With the exception of Forbes, whom he described as 'a brick – worth fifty of the others,' McDonald was greatly disparaging of the correspondents at Plymouth.

At 10.50 p.m. Shaw Savill's Plymouth agents bundled the three men into the first-class carriage of a special train bound for London. Accompanied by Forbes and other London and provincial pressmen, their story was telegraphed to all parts of the country when the train reached Exeter at 1 a.m. on the first day of 1875. Britain was experiencing its worst winter in living memory and in the atrocious conditions heralding the New Year further progress was slow. The train reached Bristol at 3.30 a.m. but it proved impossible to go on. Dressed only in light clothing given to them by the St Helena shipping master, the bemused survivors found themselves standing on a station platform one foot deep in snow and lashed by an icy wind. Despite the late hour, a railway porter found the men a hotel room, and their journey did not resume until 7 a.m. By this time the news from Exeter had established them as celebrities, and their carriage was mobbed at several stops along the route. They arrived at Paddington at 10.45 a.m. and were immediately taken to Shaw Savill's offices in Leadenhall Street.

As their horse-drawn coach made its way through the streets of London, the house belonging to the parents of emigrant Bill Eagles was pointed out to them. Eagles was a labourer who had died in McDonald's lifeboat and Cotter, himself a Londoner and overjoyed to be home, was only momentarily subdued by the reminder. On arrival at 34 Leadenhall Street, the men were greeted by James Temple, a managing owner of the *Cospatrick*, and the man who was to become the public face of Shaw, Savill & Co. in the ensuing days. Two days earlier, at the head of a deputation of influential shipowners, emigration agents, and merchants, he had lobbied London's Lord Mayor, with the result that a relief fund was set up to aid the dependent relatives and families of those who had died.[22]

Temple first made sure that the survivors were properly fed and fitted out in winter clothing before subjecting them to a lengthy interrogation. By now aware of the principal facts relating to the disaster, he focused much of his questioning on why the *Cospatrick*'s boats had failed so badly. An exhaustive account of their capabilities was drawn from McDonald, who was discomforted by having to admit that neither lifeboat was carrying water or provisions. The water kegs had, he said, been taken out of the boats the day before the fire and not replaced. Nor could he adequately explain why the boats were also lacking sails and balers. He handed Temple a watch inscribed with the name R. or A. Scott, a ring from the finger of the ship's baker, Peter Cope, and about £30 in cash, which he said had been collected from the pockets of the dead. When he suggested that the fire had originated in the boatswain's locker, Temple countered by asking whether it had started in the vessel's lower hold during an attempt by sailors to plunder cargo. This possibility was emphatically denied by McDonald, who voiced his belief in the integrity of *Cospatrick*'s seamen – but he had to concede that the beer stowed in the forward part of the hold (there were 184 barrels in all) could well have been a tempting target to thirsty men after two months at sea. The possibility that the fire had been caused as a consequence of the seamen pillaging cargo was to surface time and again during the following days and, in some minds at least, it became an established fact.

Cotter and McDonald recounted the names of the people in the two lifeboats as best they could. Strangely, both could better recollect the occupants of Charles Romaine's boat, in which they had spent a few hours, than those of the starboard boat in which they had spent nine days. They spoke of the presence of Frederick Bentley and the boy Maher (either Michael or Bartholomew) in the starboard lifeboat, but were unable to name a third boy. Cotter referred to him as a 'country boy, a rosy-cheeked little fellow' while, contrariwise, McDonald said only that 'he was a big boy'. Cotter then recounted a story of how Thomas Bentley after improbably discovering a fragment of biscuit in the bottom of the boat had given it to Frederick to eat. In what might be a reflection of the importance of children in Victorian society, they failed to mention any of the other 120 or so emigrant children on the *Cospatrick*; nor were they referred to in subsequent accounts. The two men were able to identify just 12 of the 23 male passengers believed to have been in the starboard lifeboat. Those named were Edward Bickersteth, Thomas Lewis (the Montgomeryshire cowman), John McBride, William Eagles, Thomas and Frederick Bentley, Jeremiah Leuchan, Benjamin Reeves, the Mahar child, John Anderson, Thomas Pascoe, and John Bunt. The name of Nicholas Birbeck of Skipton was subsequently added to the list by McDonald, and the watch he gave to Temple suggests that Robert Scott from Ayr was also in the boat.[23] Considering the circumstances under which the adult members of the group gained places, it is not surprising that all were young, and presumably strong, at least at the time they entered the water. After *Cospatrick*'s abandonment, 25-year-old Cornish miner John Bunt and his wife Sarah spent what was left of the night clinging to a spar, but at dawn Sarah weakened, lost her grip and drowned. By the time that Bunt and the others had secured places in the recovered lifeboat they too were near to exhaustion.

On 2 January the Receiver of Wreck, J.C. Stockton, separately subjected the survivors to examination under oath.[24] Much of Stockton's investigation was concerned with the way *Cospatrick* had been fitted out and her cargo stowed, the quality of her crew, the safety procedures on board and the manner in which the fire had been fought. By now the constraints on Cotter's tongue had wholly disappeared. He offered key evidence as to the seat of the blaze when he said that, on awakening, he saw smoke curling through the cracks in the planking between the forecastle and the fore-scuttle, and could smell ropes and tar burning. He told Stockton that on raising the alarm the emigrants had shouted out that the fire had started in the boatswain's locker. The boatswain often sent men into the locker to bring up ropes or anything else that was wanted, and on the two occasions Cotter had worked there himself he had taken a safety lantern down. The lantern was lit on deck and its flame carefully shielded to prevent accidental contact with flammable material. Such a lamp was not an obvious ignition source but, since the locker was directly beneath the forecastle and contained quantities of flammable ship's stores, Cotter was sure that the fire had originated there.[25]

McDonald provided Stockton with a detailed account of the voyage out and subsequent events. He re-stated his opinion that the fire had started in the boatswain's locker, but like Cotter was unable to suggest a likely source of ignition. Lewis, although yet to recover his mental equilibrium, took pains to defend his dead shipmates against the slur of cargo pillaging. He swore that he had never seen any of them 'the worse for liquor' and considered them 'a good serviceable crew, steady and always attentive to their duties'.[26] Lewis was still coming to terms with recent events, and through much of the hearing appeared dazed and sat muttering to himself.

Once Stockton's inquiry was over, the survivors were further examined before the New Zealand Agent-General, Isaac Featherstone. They were questioned by Edward Smith, the New Zealand official who four months earlier had overseen *Cospatrick*'s despatch from London. Smith was a former Royal Navy officer and considered knowledgeable in matters of maritime safety. He first reflected on the possibility that spontaneous combustion of the coal in the forepeak might have caused the fire, but discarded the idea because the amount involved – perhaps 30 tons – was thought insufficient to allow the necessary build-up of heat.[27] He then put it to McDonald that his theory that the fire had started in the boatswain's locker was 'absolutely untenable'. Smith suggested that the fire must have

№ 1509 Glasgow 27th Jany 75

Messrs Shaw Savill & co

Gentlemen

Yours of the 25th came duly to hand. their was beer in barrels before the main hatch. & beaft the forehatch. the Paraffin oil for Ships use was kept in the port quarter gallery. their was a very small quantity of Paint mixed by the boatswin a couple of days before the disaster for to paint the life boats

Yours Respectfully
Henry McDonald

Letter from Henry McDonald to Shaw, Savill & Co. regarding stowage of *Cospatrick*'s cargo and boatswain's stores.

originated in the forward section of the lower hold, since it would not have spread so rapidly otherwise. McDonald was taken aback by the re-emergence of this issue – everything that the survivors had seen and heard pointed to the locker being the seat of the blaze, with the fire then spreading rapidly through the 'tween deck spaces. Smith's model for the progress of the fire required a raging inferno among the 'combustibles' in *Cospatrick*'s lower hold, with the vessel being destroyed from the hold upwards. Although there was no certainty the fire had evolved in this way Smith was dismissive of likely alternatives. It was true that fire was first manifested by smoke issuing from the fore-scuttle, but this would have occurred irrespective of whether the forepeak, the fore-hold or the boatswain's locker had been the seat of the blaze.

An almost continuous trail of flammable material had extended from the locker to the farthest reaches of the lower hold. The locker itself contained quantities of varnish, turpentine, linseed and colza oils, together with pitch and tar. Beneath the locker were the coals in the forepeak while in the hold, immediately behind the forward bulkhead, were more coals, on top of which were stowed turpentine and oil in cans. Aft of these items, resting alongside the ship's water tanks and salt provisions, were stowed pitch and tar in barrels. Next came more oil, other general cargo, 25 casks of rum and several barrels of varnish. Further aft, about 50 feet from the forward bulkhead, was the consignment of beer in barrels; the barrels were stacked in tiers extending across the width of the hold and rising almost to the level of the deck above. Because of gaps between barrels and spaces above them, the arrangement would not have acted as a firewall. Iron and cement were stowed in the mid-section of the lower hold, but were covered over with emigrants' luggage and dry stores for the ship's use. These too would have burned readily. The aftermost section of the hold, extending all the way back to the sternpost, contained the remainder of the alcoholic beverages, including 1500 cases of spirits. Considering the accelerant properties of many of the items, a fire in the cargo space was certain to sweep rapidly along its length.

If the fire had started in the boatswain's locker, two pathways were available for its ready transmission to the lower hold. First, the casks of flammable matter stowed in the locker would not have remained intact for long. Once ruptured, gravity would ensure that the blazing liquid contents were carried into the bilges and the hold itself. A second path extended from the locker to the single men's quarters by way of the ventilation grill in the forward bulkhead. Once established in the 'tween deck, the fire could enter the hold by penetrating the main deck hatches. Although normally kept closed and locked, the hatches were constructed of two-inch thick pine planks covered over with the oiled canvas fabric known as tarpaulin; their resistance to burning was much less than that of the main deck teak planking. Smith, however, would not concede that a fire centred outside the cargo space could have easily gained access to the hold: 'The [main] deck would take a tremendous time to burn through,' he argued; 'it was four and a half inches thick, I don't see how the fire could have got into the lower hold unless it originated there.'[28] Since Smith also believed that 'nine tenths of the fires that occur in the hold arise through attempts by sailors to plunder cargo', the accusation against *Cospatrick*'s seamen was unmistakable.

Unobserved entry to the lower hold could only have been achieved by way of the forepeak, which was itself accessed from the fore-scuttle on the forecastle head. There was no ladder in the fore-scuttle shaft; anyone going into the forepeak did so by lowering himself down the shaft at the end of a rope. A trapdoor in the shaft at the level of the main deck was designed to isolate the forepeak from the boatswain's locker above. Three inches thick, the wooden trapdoor was normally kept shut and locked, but locks can be broken and whether the trapdoor was open or closed when the fire started is not known. Although the forward bulkhead provided a barrier to direct access to the hold from the forepeak, it was not a permanent construction, being made up of planks two-and-a-half inches thick, laid horizontally across the width of the vessel and nailed into place with the nail heads facing forward. It was said – although McDonald later offered a contrary view – that a few minutes' work with a hammer would have created an opening. The seamen having greatest access to the forepeak were the boatswain, William Symons, and Thomas Pillow, a 20-year-old ordinary seaman. Each day Pillow, 'a steady, intelligent young man' according to McDonald, went into the forepeak to get coal for the ship's galley stove and distillation plant. The coal was shovelled into baskets and then hauled to the deck by male emigrants. Pillow never took a lamp or naked flame into the forepeak, but worked by the small amount of natural light that found its way down the shaft. At night, because of the location of the fore-scuttle, it would have been possible for a person to enter the shaft without being seen. Despite Smith's assertions, McDonald remained adamant that none of *Cospatrick*'s sailors had tried to break into the hold. 'They could not get at the beer,' he told Featherstone; 'I can very nearly … swear that could not have been the case.' He added that he had been down the fore-hatch 'pretty often' over the course of the voyage and would have detected any attempt to break through the forward bulkhead.[29]

Stress was building in *Cospatrick*'s late second mate. When not attending the various investigations into the disaster, most of his time was spent at Shaw Savill's premises meeting with friends and relatives of *Cospatrick*'s emigrants and seamen. They flocked to Leadenhall Street in the hope of receiving encouraging news but, with none to be had, there were many distressing scenes. With the events of Plymouth still fresh in his mind, McDonald tried to avoid contact with the press, but was pestered to distraction by a representative of *The Times*, who followed him everywhere – harassing him even as he took meals at his lodgings.[30] On 4 January the survivors received what they were owed from Shaw, Savill & Co., and were placed on the payroll of the Board of Trade. This arrangement allowed their pay to continue until the official Board of Trade inquiry into *Cospatrick*'s loss was complete. On the evening of 5 January, with the date for this final inquiry still to be set, McDonald left by train for Montrose. Toward the end of the journey he was met at Guthrie Junction by his wife, Jane, and brother, Osmond. He remained oppressed by memories of the wreck, and Jane soon realised that the husband she had last seen four months earlier was not the man he once was.[31]

7. Aftermath

The Board of Trade did urge ship-owners to adopt fire drills, to exercise the crews for lowering boats, as well as to provide their boats with oars, rudders and provisions at all times; but there was no law empowering them to enforce any regulations.

Sir Charles Adderley, President of the Board of Trade,
responding to a question in the House of Commons on 22 February 1875

At the beginning of 1875 the Board of Trade was feeling the full weight of its maritime responsibilities. As the board's marine department struggled to cope with inquiries into an unprecedented number of known shipwrecks, its president, Sir Charles Adderley, faced increasingly awkward questions on matters of maritime safety in the House of Commons. Many of these concerned the seaworthiness of ten British steamships, posted as missing during the previous four months and which were now presumed lost. The *Cospatrick* disaster was therefore just one of the issues confronting the maritime community at this time. Samuel Plimsoll's campaign to remove unseaworthy ships from the British Merchant Marine was intensifying, and he remained a thorn in the side of the government. Adderley, who had wished 'to leave unfettered the self-dependence and elasticity of our mercantile marine', was now forced to acknowledge that 'the eager competition of mercantile enterprise [has] been reckless of human life'. But although pushed into admitting the need for reform, the procrastinating Adderley failed to address the major concerns – 'some of the most important are not ripe for immediate legislation,' he announced to the House on 8 February.[1] Others held different views, but the Board of Trade was unwilling to act.

It was in this climate of bureaucratic lethargy that Shaw Savill's James Temple attempted to forestall a public outcry over the safety standards on the *Cospatrick*. 'Shaw Savill and other companies engaged in like business', he said, 'had always done all that lay in their power to secure the safety of passengers carried by their vessels, and [would] accept any reasonable and practicable suggestion with a view to secure greater safety to emigrants.'[2] Although there is little evidence to suggest that Shaw Savill had ever made emigrant safety a priority, Temple's statement did succeed in attracting suggestions, both practicable and otherwise.[3] Chemists proposed that wooden emigrant vessels should be 'fire-proofed', either by coating the ships' timbers with fire-retardant chemicals, or soaking them to complete saturation in a concentrated solution of alum – although what effect these treatments might have on the health of emigrants cooped up in the 'tween decks seemed not to be a consideration. Captain Paul Boynton, an American safety specialist, took the opportunity to promote his recently invented 'life-saving dress'. Made of rubber, Boynton's two-piece inflatable garment was a forerunner of the modern wet suit. 'It would,' he said, 'render the wearer insubmergible and buoyant as a cork.' However, he failed to explain how the suit might have been used on the *Cospatrick*. A letter published in *The Times* advocated that Australia- and New Zealand-bound emigrant ships should sail in company throughout the entire passage, a difficult proposition given the demanding weather of the Southern Ocean. Throughout January, letters on the subject of maritime safety streamed into the offices of British newspapers; many offered commonsense views to the effect that the carriage of flammable liquids on emigrant ships should be restricted, and the provisioning of boats and the holding of boat and fire drills made compulsory. The Admiral of the Fleet, George Sartorius, wrote to recommend that ships should be divided into compartments, with arrangements allowing each to be flooded in the event of fire. Furthermore, if these measures were thought insufficient, 'convenient parts of the vessel' might be adapted to allow them to be used as rafts, 'equally available for saving life in case of wreck or fire.' The convenient parts of the vessel Sartorius had in mind were cabin tops and deck sections, which, if filled with cork, might float off should the vessel sink. Irrespective of practicality, such suggestions guaranteed that public attention was drawn to the Board of Trade inquiry into *Cospatrick*'s loss when this opened on 3 February.

Held at the Greenwich Police Court, the hearing was presided over by Stipendiary Magistrate James Henry Patteson and three nautical assessors: Captains Charles Pryce and John Castle, and William Henry Turner, the principal shipwright-surveyor of the Board of Trade. Shaw, Savill & Co., the New Zealand Government, and the Board of Trade were represented by counsel, but no such facility was afforded *Cospatrick*'s seamen – or, for that matter, the relatives of the ship's dead emigrants. John Castle was particularly well qualified to investigate fire at sea. In 1857 he had commanded the iron troopship *Sarah Sands* during an epic battle with fire in the Indian Ocean.[4] In the 24 hours it took to extinguish the blaze, every item of woodwork aft of the main-mast was consumed and the deck-beams and hull plating were left warped and twisted. Despite this massive damage, the *Sarah Sands* remained afloat and Castle was able to navigate her safely to Mauritius.

Lacking physical evidence of the wreck, the *Cospatrick* inquiry laboured under difficulties similar to those of a coroner's inquest in the absence of a body. Apart from the testimony of the survivors, the only evidence available to the court were details of the vessel's construction and equipment, and the composition of the cargo and the manner of its stowage. Undeterred by the paucity of information, Patteson and his colleagues pronounced their aim as two-fold: first to establish the cause of the fire, and second – and this goal was set without any hint of irony – to determine whether the vessel had sufficient boats, and whether they had been correctly used with 'proper precautions taken to prevent their being overcrowded.'[5]

Cotter and Lewis were called but could add little to the facts previously placed before the Receiver of Wreck. Opening remarks by counsel for the Board of Trade, Arthur Cohen QC, centred on the propriety of sending out emigrants on a ship laden with inflammable merchandise, and whether Shaw Savill had been negligent in this regard. *Cospatrick*'s final clearance from Gravesend had included the astonishing declaration that there were no combustibles in the cargo. Once this was known, in January 1875, Captain John Forster, the Board of Trade officer responsible for issuing the clearance, was immediately taken to task by T.H. Farrer, the board's permanent secretary. Farrer demanded that Forster 'write at once to report fully how it was that your Certificate was not in accordance with the facts, if spirits and turpentine are not combustible – what is?'[6] However, Forster's declaration, although totally misleading, fully complied with the law as it then stood. Board of Trade officers responsible for despatching emigrant ships were not required to regard substances such as wood, turpentine, petroleum-based solvents, and proof spirits as combustible and potentially dangerous. Although *Cospatrick*'s cargo had contained these items in plenty, they were not seen as improper.[7] But proper or not, even the managing stevedore responsible for stowing the vessel had to fully agree with Cohen's proposition that the freight 'could not be better arranged to burn, and would make a capital fire'.[8] The nature of the cargo and boatswain's stores, and the absence of permanent dividing bulkheads, made the rapid spread of a fire inevitable. As with so many other ships of the day, the *Cospatrick*, built of wood to an open plan and loaded with materials of varying degrees of flammability, was tinder waiting for a spark.

But what had supplied the spark and where had it fallen? McDonald, who had returned from Scotland to attend the inquiry, reiterated his belief that the fire had originated in the boatswain's locker. Under questioning by Captains Pryce and Castle, he emphasised the quality of *Cospatrick*'s crew and denied the possibility that they had caused the fire while pillaging cargo. Access to the fore-hold was prevented by forward bulkhead, which, he said, 'was very strong and lined with tin'. Perhaps the fire had started when an emigrant in the single men's compartment, in fear of being caught smoking below decks, had discarded a match or pipe ash into the locker through the ventilation grill? The grill had mesh 'large enough for a man's hand' and any item tossed through would either fall down the fore-scuttle shaft to the forepeak, or lodge among the combustibles in the locker. Installed during the vessel's fitting out at the behest of the New Zealand despatching officer Edward Smith, the ventilation grill had allowed the blaze to enter the 'tween deck unhindered. It was now suggested as an additional weakness that had made the initial outbreak possible.

This scenario, entirely plausible, was considered by the court and rejected. Little significance was placed on the fire-accelerating properties of the stores contained in the boatswain's locker. Moreover, there was an unwonted confidence that the night watchmen stationed at the three main hatchways had been diligent. If the blaze had started in the locker, surely the watchmen would have discovered it before it had gained such a hold over the vessel?

Despite the course taken in his earlier questioning of McDonald, James

Temple of Shaw Savill was another who doubted the fire had originated in the hold. While not called on to present his views directly, he argued through counsel that the absence of positive evidence in favour of cargo pillaging meant that no finding should be made against either crew or emigrants. Although there was a complete lack of certainty regarding the time that the lower hold had become involved in the fire, Edward Smith's view held sway: 'The fire came from plunder,' Smith told the court on the third and final day of the hearing; 'it never could have originated in the boatswain's locker, for it could not have got into the lower hold as soon as it did.'[9] Arthur Cohen had argued along similar lines and Magistrate Patteson and his assessors agreed. In their unanimous opinion, the fire must have started in the lower hold; and, since spontaneous combustion was unlikely, the source of ignition must have been a lucifer match or candle dropped during an attempt to broach cargo. Either a sailor or an emigrant had entered the hold after first removing the planks of the forward bulkhead, and had accidentally set fire to straw or some other inflammable material. Since the fore-scuttle was open at the time, the inquiry concluded that 'the smoke and flames would probably be drawn to that spot, where they would come in contact with the tar, oil, varnish, pitch &c., … rendering any attempt to get the fire under to prove of little or no avail.'[10] It was a finding easily reached. With blame laid squarely on the shoulders of the emigrants and sailors, the court had avoided calling into question the system under which emigration was conducted and the inherently dangerous nature of 'colonial cargoes'.

Having thus satisfied itself as to the cause of the fire, the court next pondered the question of the boats. Experiments conducted on the emigrant ship *Tintern Abbey* just four weeks earlier had supplied an answer. The *Tintern Abbey* had sailed from Gravesend for New Zealand on 6 January, with boats sufficient for only one half of the 378 people she was carrying. Although the ship's two lifeboats were adequately provisioned and had performed passably well in tests, some of the safety equipment was not up to Board of Trade standards. All the deficiencies of boats stowed on skids were revealed: 'It taxed the resources of one quarter of the crew (which numbered 46) to get the port pinnace off in a quarter of an hour,' an observer reported.[11] The *Abbey*'s pinnace was stowed keel-up and, despite the men working with a will, 'inspirited [by] their usual quaint songs when it came to the hauling', it took six minutes to get the craft upright and a further nine before it was hoisted over the side and lowered into the water – all this in broad daylight as the vessel lay stationary in calm water.[12] Substantially more time would have been needed had the experiment included filling the boat with passengers. McDonald told the court that the same series of operations with *Cospatrick*'s longboat would have required 20 minutes. Except for the captain's gig, he said, none of *Cospatrick*'s boats had been off their skids in the six months he was on the ship.

And at least one boat may have been totally unsound. Years after the inquiry, Cotter was reported as saying that the port cutter, one of the two boats carried on skids forward, was holed and 'so rotten as to be useless'.[13] He failed to mention this when giving evidence in 1875 but, taken with the fact that much of the equipment in the two lifeboats was missing, it increases the suspicion that even by the relaxed standards of the day the *Cospatrick* was poorly prepared for an encounter with misfortune. Was Captain Elmslie aware of unsoundness among the boats? If so, did the knowledge contribute to his reluctance to have them provisioned and readied for launching while there was still time? Elmslie's state of mind is difficult to fathom. Undoubtedly brave, he was said to be 'careful and particular' and meticulous in his attention to detail.[14] The presence of his wife and child on *Cospatrick* might reasonably be expected to have reinforced these traits, but he was surprisingly complacent on matters of safety.

Patteson's inquiry handed down its findings on 11 February. Fixed on the idea that communication between the forepeak and the lower hold should be impossible, it recommended that wooden passenger vessels should be fitted with a forward bulkhead 'as strong as the ingenuity of shipwrights can suggest'. This, the court's only recommendation concerning changes to ship fittings, was not particularly far-reaching in 1875, when ship design had progressed to the point where forward collision bulkheads were incorporated as a matter of course. Extraordinarily, the court passed over the fact that *Cospatrick*'s six boats had proved totally inadequate for the purpose of saving life. Patteson himself appears to have been reluctant to probe the state of the ship's safety equipment, and during the inquiry was heard to remark:

'Nobody doubts that the *Cospatrick* was a splendid vessel.'[15] However, the court did conclude that the practice of stowing boats keel uppermost was 'most objectionable' and suggested that these were better stowed upright on chocks. Significantly, it recommended that 'all ships carrying passengers or emigrants should be compelled to exercise their crews weekly, weather permitting, at fire and boat stations, and that an entry should be made in the official log certifying that such had been done.'[16] Had this suggestion been implemented, the deaths of 476 of *Cospatrick*'s complement might not have been in vain, but in 1875 the political will to carry it forward was lacking. Thirty-one more years were to pass before it became compulsory to hold regular boat drills on British passenger vessels.

The finding that *Cospatrick*'s destruction was a consequence of cargo pillaging caused widespread dismay. It was one thing to lose a ship and almost its entire complement through the forces of nature, but quite another for the loss to have resulted from criminal action. Cargo plundering was said to be epidemic in ships making the long haul from Britain to New Zealand. Many carried large volumes of beer and spirits in their lower hold, commodities seen as fair game by poorly disciplined men after many weeks at sea. And as offenders invariably used naked flames – candles or lucifer matches – to light their way in the pitch-black cargo spaces, the risk of fire was enormous. If an outward-bound vessel was posted missing, the immediate suspicion was that sailors had set it on fire while attempting to broach cargo. The issue particularly concerned the New Zealand Government, not least because it added to what were hazards enough for prospective migrants. When Britons learned of the loss of the *Cospatrick*, the number of assisted emigrants departing for New Zealand fell sharply. Fewer than one thousand left for the colony during the first two months of 1875, whereas more than twice that number had departed in December 1874 alone.[17]

New Zealand's Premier, Julius Vogel, first heard of the disaster while on a visit to Europe. Realising that it placed New Zealand's immigration scheme under threat, he was 'greatly excited by the affair and telegraphed from Florence like a house burning!'[18] On learning the conclusions of Patteson's inquiry, he questioned whether the penalty for broaching cargo (up to three months' jail, with or without hard labour, according to the provisions of the Merchant Shipping Act) was sufficient punishment for a crime that placed hundreds of lives at risk. In letters to the Colonial Office and the Board of Trade written in April and May of 1875, he argued that 'the case of emigrant ships is fraught with such horrible consequences, that as a necessary precaution scarcely any punishment could be too heavy for it.'[19] Vogel was well aware that acts of plunder on New Zealand-bound ships were not only widespread but so flagrant as to amount to mutiny. In 1874 there were at least three instances (*Tweed*, *Queen of the Age*, and *Cathcart* were the vessels involved) when attempts to control cargo plundering met with such insubordination that ships' officers took up arms in self-defence. Discipline on *Cathcart* deteriorated so sharply after her seamen got to the spirits that the captain shot and wounded three during efforts to restore order. Vogel's representations soon ensured that the worst cases of cargo pillaging were treated as larceny – an offence attracting the harsher penalty of either three years' penal servitude or two years' jail with hard labour – and from February 1876 offenders brought before New Zealand courts were dealt with under the stricter regime. But given the nature of the problem, an increased level of punishment was no real substitute for stout bulkheads and secure cargo hatches. The downturn in the number of New Zealand-bound emigrants proved short lived and Vogel's target of 25,000 for the whole of 1875 was easily achieved.

While Vogel agitated to secure increased penalties for cargo plundering, the New Zealand Agent-General Isaac Featherstone sought to strengthen the regulations governing the carriage of dangerous cargoes on New Zealand-bound emigrant ships. It was some time before the lesson of the *Cospatrick* sank in, and throughout 1875 vessels continued to leave Britain's shores with passengers and dangerous goods in close proximity. Shaw Savill was fortunate not to lose the chartered iron barque *Lutterworth* on 20 June, when fire was discovered behind wood panelling in the storeroom. Bound for Auckland, the *Lutterworth* was carrying 35 passengers and a cargo that included 40 tons of explosives, 30 tons of lucifer matches, and other 'combustibles'. Understandably, these items provided a huge incentive to quell the fire, which was fought with 'the energy of despair' until extinguished.[20] The crew of the *Strathmore* (also a Shaw, Savill & Co. vessel) broached cargo to such effect during a voyage from London to

Photographs of the *Cospatrick* (see page 23) are advertised for sale in Otago after her loss becomes known. (*Otago Daily Times*, 1875)

Otago in April 1875 that 'all were drunk excepting five, so the passengers were obliged to assist them'. Strangely enough this information came to light after the *Strathmore* was posted as missing, but only because it was contained in a letter handed to a passing ship in May.[21] It was therefore natural to assume that *Strathmore* had been destroyed as a consequence of cargo pillaging (30 tons of explosives were on board), whereas the vessel, which was carrying 50 passengers, had stranded on the remote Crozet Islands in the Indian Ocean. The true cause of the loss – which occurred during the night of 30 June – was discovered only when the survivors were rescued from the Crozets in January 1876. Reacting to these and similar incidents, Featherstone hastened to reassure prospective emigrants that 'no … commodity likely to be detrimental to the safety or health of the passengers shall be taken as cargo or otherwise, and that this provision is strictly enforced by me.'[22]

Strathmore and *Lutterworth* were able to carry dangerous goods because under the regulations of the time neither was classified as a 'passenger ship'. For economic reasons this designation, with its attendant restrictions on the type of cargo that could be carried, was not bestowed until passenger numbers exceeded a certain liberal threshold based on vessel tonnage. The nineteenth-century practice of sending vessels to sea with passengers and dangerous goods in close combination was acceptable to both insurers and shipowners, but travellers were often unaware of what lay in the hold beneath their feet.

In Auckland, concern over *Cospatrick*'s non-appearance had increased daily after the arrival of the barque *Glenlora* on 5 January 1875. *Glenlora*'s passage from London had taken 101 days and, as she had left port 15 days after the *Cospatrick*, it was apparent that all was not well. When news of the disaster eventually reached Auckland on 11 January, its impact was as great as in any region of Britain.[23] Twenty of *Cospatrick*'s emigrants had been nominated to travel out by friends or relatives living either in or near the city, and many others were also well known locally. A special edition of the *Evening Star* newspaper was printed and distributed: 'the sad intelligence was left at residences in the outskirts of the city, in many cases the back of the messenger was scarcely turned when a wail of anguish told how the tidings had come home.'[24] Auckland was in mourning for weeks.

In a curious sequel to the *Cospatrick* disaster, the New Zealand Government took action against Shaw, Savill & Co. to recover half the money it had paid as fares for the vessel's emigrants. The sum being sought amounted to £2562 17s 6d. Somewhat surprisingly, the matter went to court despite the charter agreement between the two parties clearly stating that the shipping company agreed to 'repay the half of the passage money for each emigrant who may have died during the voyage, or have left the ship prior to arriving at the port of disembarkation'.[25] Shaw Savill's reluctance to settle was based on a belief that liability extended only to cases where lives had been lost through illness, but this weak defence was not accepted. The judgement, handed down by the Queen's Bench Division of the High Court of Justice on 1 February 1876, found uniformly in favour of the plaintiff and in early April the company paid in full.

The eventual fate of McDonald's lifeboat is unknown. The boat was 24 $^1/_2$ feet long, 6 $^3/_4$ wide and 2 $^3/_4$ deep, and was rated to hold 30 adults, but as many as 100 people, possibly more, had died in and around the craft during a single 10-day period. Nearly 80 people, mainly women, drowned after being tipped into the sea when the boat's davits collapsed, and a further 25 – men and boys – died during its subsequent northward drift off the coast of Southern Africa. William Jahnke had the boat hoisted on board *British Sceptre* when he rescued *Cospatrick*'s survivors, and it was off-loaded with them at St Helena. Its interior may well have been restored,

The *Cospatrick* memorial at Shipton-under-Wychwood. The tree behind the memorial commemorates the centenary of the disaster.

allowing it to be put to further use; Shaw Savill's *Dover Castle* was reported to be carrying the lifeboat at the time of her visit to Auckland in August 1875,[26] and, if so, it was probably still on board when the vessel was sold to Norwegian interests in 1881.

The only lasting monument of the *Cospatrick* disaster is located many miles from the sea in the small Oxfordshire village of Shipton-under-Wychwood. The unpretentious stone memorial was erected on the village green in 1878 and paid for by local subscription. It commemorates the 17 Shipton residents, comprising three generations of the Townsend and

Hedges families, who died on the *Cospatrick*. Henry Townsend and Richard Hedges were two of the oldest men on the ship, and had been encouraged in their decision to emigrate by a family member already in New Zealand. Both men were agricultural workers, whose resolve to leave Shipton would certainly have been hardened by the tense situation surrounding labour relations in Oxfordshire in the months before departure. In April 1872 the newly formed Oxford District Branch of the National Agricultural Labourers Union had begun attempts to secure better pay and conditions for local rural workers, but these met with strong resistance from employers. Lock-outs became commonplace and matters were brought to a head at nearby Ascott-under-Wychwood in May 1873, when several wives and daughters of striking farm workers were arrested for intimidating two men employed to act as strike-breakers. Sixteen of the women, two with children at breast, were found to have contravened a regulation aimed at restricting picketing, and local magistrates (both clerics and not impartial) sentenced them to several days in jail with hard labour.[27] This affair, known as the Chipping Norton Case, created a national scandal, and may have done as much to encourage migration from Oxfordshire as the loss of the Shipton seventeen did to deter it. Following the sinking of the *Cospatrick* local interest in emigration decreased dramatically, but this coincided with an increasing awareness of union strength and significant improvements to wage rates and conditions of employment for Oxfordshire farm workers.[28] Migration from Britain as a whole was not greatly affected by the loss of the emigrant ship – after all, many had been lost before – and the number of Britons leaving scarcely altered.

In the quarter of a century immediately following the *Cospatrick* disaster, the British merchant shipping industry changed almost beyond recognition. Ship design and construction methods were transformed when steel superseded iron and timber as building material, and huge improvements were made to the reliability and fuel efficiency of the steam engine. Steam-powered vessels increasingly dominated the shipping lanes – in 1874 sailing vessels made up around 70 per cent of UK-registered shipping tonnage, but by 1899 this figure had dropped to 25 per cent. Over the same period the British merchant fleet expanded from a total of 5.9 million registered tons to 9.2 million registered tons.[29] This growth was accompanied by a rapid increase in the average size of passenger vessels, but official thinking on maritime life-saving equipment was slow to adapt. The changes that were made reflected a mindset locked into the thinking of Clause 27 of the 1855 Passengers Act. In particular, tonnage, rather than the number of people on board, remained as the factor determining the minimum number of boats a passenger ship should carry. This philosophy, less satisfactory with each year that passed, inevitably increased the potential scale for disaster at sea.

The point was inadvertently illustrated by Sir Digby Murray, Professional Member of the Marine Department of the Board of Trade, when he appeared before the Select Committee for Saving Life at Sea in 1887. Murray had little confidence in ships' boats, believing them incapable of saving the lives of passengers 'in even moderately bad weather [as they] would infallibly be swamped or capsized before they got clear of the ship.' And if some combination of weather and good fortune allowed them to be safely launched, then: 'the first gale will swamp them … Steamships,' he told the committee, 'should carry as many boats as their dimensions render reasonable and practicable.'[30] At this time *every* passenger ship of 1500 tons or more fully complied with the law if it was equipped with seven boats; owners could increase the number of boats if they wished, but there was no compulsion to do so. Murray cited the case of the 3888-ton White Star Line steamship *Adriatic*, which carried 1251 passengers and crew while being equipped with eight boats with the capacity to hold just 250 people. *Adriatic*'s decks could have easily accommodated more boats, but Murray, in an abrupt shift in logic, did not favour increasing the vessel's life-saving capability. Instead he used the example of the *Adriatic* as an argument for not reducing the number of lifeboats on larger ships better endowed. *Adriatic* was entirely representative of White Star Line steamships of the 1880s, which on average had a lifeboat capacity sufficient for just 20 per cent of the people being carried.[31] Even so, one boat-place for every five persons was hardly the end of the spectrum.

When the 686 ton British steamer *Sir John Lawrence* was lost with all hands after sailing into a cyclone off Calcutta on 25 May 1887, her boats were rated as able to hold just 98 of the 776 passengers and crew said to have been on board.[32] And even this life-saving capacity may have been overestimated, as one of the vessel's two lifeboats was reported to be 'utterly useless, and leaking so badly that all efforts to make it watertight failed.'[33] Allegations about the state of the boat and corrosion in the *Sir John Lawrence*'s hull plating were made before the ensuing Court of Inquiry by two former crew members, Chief Officer William Neustein and Chief Engineer John Leech, both of whom had been sacked by the ship's owners a few months before the vessel foundered. The court chose to dismiss their claims – this despite the *Sir John Lawrence* having been passed as seaworthy by a Board of Trade surveyor known to be in the pay of her owners, and Neustein raising concerns about the condition of the vessel well before the beginning of the fatal voyage. With all the evidence lying at the bottom of the sea, there was no refuting the decision. The court had no confidence in the figure finally arrived at as the death toll, since it emerged that the *Sir John Lawrence* commonly (and unlawfully) carried between 1300 and 1400 passengers. As there had been no formal ticketing arrangement for passengers the estimate of the number lost was at best a guess, and in the court's view 'the alleged counting of passengers previous to the departure of the vessel from Calcutta was little better than a mockery and a show.'[34] The official toll of 776 is therefore best regarded as a minimum figure. Peter Irvine, the *Sir John Lawrence*'s captain, was almost certainly lining his own pockets by engaging in an illicit traffic of passengers, but why he deliberately took his vessel into what was a storm of unparalleled ferocity is less easy to understand. In the opinion of the court this was 'an act of foolhardiness, almost criminal in its nature'.[35] The sinking of the *Sir John Lawrence* attracted little attention in Britain, mainly because most of the dead were Hindus and disasters in the 'Far East' were so remote as not to be newsworthy. However, in terms of lives lost, the foundering of this nondescript coastal trader rates as the worst British merchant marine incident of the nineteenth century.

Despite Sir Digby Murray's representations, the 1887 Select Committee for Saving Life at Sea concluded that all sea-going passenger ships should be compelled to carry boats and life-saving gear 'as would in aggregate best provide for the safety of all on board in moderate weather'.[36] In reaching this opinion the committee had been strongly influenced by arguments presented by Thomas Gray. Gray, whose career with the Marine Department of the Board of Trade extended back to

1854, had his finger on the pulse of the merchant shipping industry; he actively promoted the training of young merchant seamen,[37] and was highly regarded for his contribution to the 'Rules of the Road' – regulations formulated with the aim of minimising the risk of collision at sea.[38] To make the complex rules more easily remembered he famously converted them to verse, to such effect that 70 years later the rhyme was still required reading for candidates taking their examination for master. Public-spirited and hard working, Gray spent his holidays at sea searching for information that would better enable him to carry out his official duties. As these brought him into regular conflict with British ship-owners, one result was that he became 'one of the best abused men in the Civil Service'.[39] A number of particularly vociferous attacks were triggered by his forthright comments on the factors contributing to loss of life at sea before a Royal Commission in 1885.[40] Awarded a CB in the same year, more considered opinion deemed him 'a jolly good fellow who deserves all he gets for his uncommon shrewdness and general ability'.[41] His standing among seafarers was enhanced by the suggestion made to the 1887 Select Committee for Saving Life at Sea that the rules relating to life-saving appliances should be framed by members of the maritime community, rather than by politicians. Gray believed that only those with a direct interest in the outcome – ship-owners and ship-builders, and Board of Trade, seamen's and Lloyd's Register representatives – should participate in their formulation.[42] This proposal was rapidly adopted, with the result that by 1890 passenger vessels of 9000 tons and above were obliged to carry at least 14 boats under davits with the capacity to accommodate a minimum of 525 people. Even at this time, however, many ship-owners were still attaching much importance to avoiding 'undue encumbrance of the ship's decks by boats'.[43] Four years later the rules were further modified, and the Merchant Shipping Act of 1894 directed that passenger vessels of 10,000 tons and above should carry a minimum of 16 lifeboats under davits with the capacity to hold at least 550.

When the 46,378-ton White Star liner *Titanic* sailed from Southampton for New York on her maiden voyage on 10 April 1912 she did so under a modification of the '10,000 ton rule' of the 1894 Act, which required her owners to provide boat accommodation for at least 962 people. *Titanic* herself was designed to carry about 3300. On board the vessel at the time of her loss after striking an iceberg on 12 April were 899 crew and 1324 passengers. *Titanic*'s 20 lifeboats (four more than the legal minimum) were rated as able to hold 1178 people, but managed to save just 705. This was 473 fewer than the boats' stated capacity, and 1518 fewer than the total number of people on board. As is now well known, all 1518 died from drowning or exposure. The circumstance of the casualty – *Titanic*, away from effective outside help, sank in a calm sea, taking three hours over the process, all the while retaining an attitude ideally suited to getting filled lifeboats into the water without mishap – was, in 1912, not considered remotely possible for a large passenger vessel. Although the disaster is remembered as one where the rescue of women and children was given priority, the gesture was tainted by a preference for privilege. Of the 156 women and children travelling as first-class passengers, no fewer than 145 were given places in *Titanic*'s lifeboats; all 145 were picked up alive, corresponding to a survival rate of 93 per cent. The women and children in the second-class accommodation had a lesser chance of being placed in a lifeboat (104 of the 128 on board were given places, 81 per cent), while for those in third-class the chance was lower again (105 of the 224 on board were given places, 47 per cent). Of the 508 women and children on the *Titanic*, 154 lost their lives.[44]

Following the loss of the huge liner, the slogan became '*Boats for All!*' Public dissatisfaction with British lifeboat legislation on both sides of the Atlantic, together with the large death toll among *Titanic*'s influential first-class male passengers, triggered changes which, decades earlier, losses like those of the *Northfleet*, the *Cospatrick*, and dozens of other vessels had failed to bring about. Within days of the disaster, White Star's management stated that the company would 'disregard technicalities … and give a most ample and complete protection to human life, in future there will never arise a condition in where there is not room for everybody in lifeboats or in unsinkable life-rafts.'[45] The concerns of other shipping companies regarding the encumbering of decks if a policy of 'Boats for All' was adopted were swept aside and, at the instigation of the Board of Trade, maritime safety legislation was belatedly given a thorough overhaul. Change was made not only to the regulations governing the carriage of lifeboats, but also to those dealing with seaborne wireless telegraphy, ship construction, navigation, and the manning of vessels. The first International Conference on Safety of Life at Sea (SOLAS) was convened in the autumn of 1913. On 20 January 1914 its recommendations, which dealt with the principal questions relating to safety of life on ocean-going passenger vessels – particularly those focusing on the issue of 'Boats for All' – were ratified by the United States, Great Britain, three British Empire and 10 European countries.[46] Article 40 of the convention declares a fundamental principle which, from 1914, has stood the test of time: 'At no moment of its voyage may a ship have on board a total number of persons greater than that for whom accommodation is provided in the lifeboats and pontoon life-rafts on board.'[47]

Henry McDonald (top),
Edward Cotter (middle)
and Thomas Lewis.

8. THREE MEN IN A BOAT

On the 5th inst., of paralysis of the brain, Charles H. McDonald, late spirit merchant, 1 Westport Dundee, and one of the three survivors (rescued by the British Sceptre) of 499 [sic] passengers and crew of ship Cospatrick, of London, which was burnt at sea on the voyage from London to Auckland, New Zealand in 1874 (Demerara papers please copy)

Death notice of (Charles) Henry McDonald,
the *Weekly News* (Dundee), 11 April 1885

Had all six boats been safely launched from the *Cospatrick*, the notional chance of a given individual obtaining a place in one would have been 38 per cent (479 persons competing for 183 places). This chance reduced to just 6 per cent (approximately 30 available places) once five of the six were out of commission, but with the recovery of the capsized starboard lifeboat the odds increased to a little over 12 per cent. As the sailors had largely decided the composition of the group occupying the port lifeboat, the chance for survival was naturally weighted in their favour; but although preferring their own kind they allowed entry of at least two children and no fewer than four small but entirely intact family groups.[1] Individual ruthlessness and physical strength was not enough to secure a place in the boat, since the seamen defended against emigrants as a cohort. However, this defence was the only organised action during the *Cospatrick*'s abandonment. By various means, 13 per cent of the ship's complement (18 members of crew or 41 per cent of the total and 44 emigrants or 10 per cent of the total) eventually found places in the ship's boats, but whether they were more fortunate than the 87 per cent who did not is a matter for conjecture.

Had Charles Romaine's craft survived the storm of 21 November 1874, its 32 occupants would have undergone the same privations as those in McDonald's boat – and with similar result. *Cospatrick*'s course had taken her well away from the shipping lanes normally used by vessels sailing to New Zealand and this drastically reduced the probability of an early rescue. The failure of McDonald's boat to make any sort of progress toward the Cape, coupled with the total absence of water and provisions, consigned its occupants to a rapid progression from debilitation to death. This progression was further accelerated by the poorly clad state of the survivors and the temperature extremes they experienced. Not surprisingly, those who were not only physically tough but could hold out the longest against the almost overwhelming temptation to drink sea water had the greatest chance of survival. Some despaired early and succumbed, while others drew strength from where they could and managed to resist; McDonald, Lewis, Cotter, and Hamilton were in the latter category. Members of the same watch and companions of sorts after weeks of working together, they sustained one another at critical times. Lewis, the eldest, was the key to keeping up the spirits of his shipmates. Competent, optimistic, and seemingly unshakeable, his was a reassuring presence. Of course, along with McDonald and Cotter, he had made the fortunate and ultimately life-saving decision to switch from the port to the starboard lifeboat. All three men were in relatively good physical condition at this time, whereas a number of their newfound companions were not; this, too, was critical in determining their survival.

Detailed information on individual nineteenth century merchant seamen is usually hard to come by. Itinerant and often poorly educated, their names (frequently spelt incorrectly) may be found on ships' articles of employment, but few records of their existence remain otherwise. *Cospatrick*'s survivors were an exception, and it has been possible to discover much about their lives.

Thomas Lewis returned to Anglesey once the Board of Trade inquiry was complete. He was welcomed into the Lewis family home at Pen-Stryd in Moelfre, where his sister Catherine Williams and her family were also living. Both parents were alive at this time, although his mother, Anne, died later in the year. Little is known of Lewis's early life, but he was 'bred a fisherman' and later saw service in the Royal Navy. On the *Cospatrick* he was sometimes referred to as 'the foreigner', seemingly because he had once worked among Belgians; to the villagers of Moelfre he was known as Tom Pen-Stryd. In his later years he found employment on various vessels sailing out of nearby Bangor, but while mate of the coaster *C.S. Atkinson* suffered a severe leg injury when a load of Welsh slate slipped from its sling and fell into the hold where he was working. The leg was amputated and the accident put an end to his seafaring. Lewis, who appears never to have married, subsequently became something of a local character in Moelfre – bearded and weather-beaten, wearing seaman's clothing and getting about the village with the aid of a wooden leg. When questioned on his boat-handling ability he once proudly responded with the Welsh language expression: '*Ni rhof fy nghap i lawr i neb!*' – a phrase which translates as: 'I will not put my cap down to anybody!'[2] By this he meant that he believed himself without peer when it came to managing small boats. But beyond Moelfre the skills that had allowed a flimsily rigged lifeboat to survive for 10 days amidst South Atlantic storms went largely unrecognised.

Lewis died of bronchitis in 1894. He is buried in the peaceful Llanallgo churchyard, where he rests in the company of generations of Anglesey's fishermen, mariners and lifeboatmen. Nearby – perhaps one mile as the

Thomas Lewis's final resting place: the Llanallgo churchyard, Anglesey.

crow flies – is the rocky headland on which the steam clipper *Royal Charter* came to grief in the early hours of 26 October 1859. Many victims of this famous sea disaster are also buried at Llanallgo. Lewis was most likely at sea at the time of *Royal Charter*'s destruction (he would then have been in his thirty-first year), but three villagers of the same surname are included in the 'Moelfre Twenty Eight' who carried out a celebrated rescue.[3] Given the small size of this close-knit community, they were almost certainly related to the man who himself achieved notoriety as a shipwreck survivor. Moelfre is a village of considerable charm, little changed since Lewis's time and retaining much of its character as a small nineteenth century fishing centre. The Pen-Stryd cottage in which he was raised and later shared with the Williams family still exists – but has been considerably modified. At the time of writing, the house was in use as a gift shop named for Lewis – 'Tom Pen-Stryd'.

Cotter also returned to the sea following the *Cospatrick* disaster. His seagoing career had begun as a boy, when he received instruction in basic seamanship on the *Chichester* training ship. *Chichester* was a redundant Royal Navy frigate, which, following representations to the Admiralty from the social reformer Lord Shaftesbury, was set up as a sea-training school at Greenhithe in 1866. Shaftesbury's two-fold purpose in creating the school was to remove the 'wild and wandering boys' from London's streets,[4] and through education and discipline turn them into sailors suitable for employment in the merchant service or the Royal Navy. Both institutions had an almost insatiable demand for seamen, and sea-training establishments were features of all Britain's major seaports. Boys accepted into *Chichester* were usually between 13 and 17 years of age, and were often orphans escaping from a background of acute deprivation. When Cotter entered the ship on 5 July 1872, he stated that his father, James, had been dead for three years, whereas census information indicates that James Cotter was still alive as late as April 1871.[5] For reasons not always apparent Cotter was often less than forthright when giving details of his personal circumstances, but may have felt that being fatherless would guarantee his admission. William Wood, another ordinary seaman on the *Cospatrick* during her final voyage, was taken into *Chichester* because his mother had died when he was six years old and his father was blind.

The training ship *Chichester* at Greenhithe on the Thames. (*The Illustrated London News*, 1867)

An occupant of Charles Romaine's lifeboat when it disappeared, Wood had once spent seven days in prison for the crime of swimming in the Thames.[6]

During their time on *Chichester*, trainees were taught seamanship and given basic schooling. This education also included a healthy component of moral and religious instruction, intended to instil Victorian virtues in boys who might later find themselves placed among what *Chichester*'s commander, Captain James Thurburn RN, termed 'misled crews of lawless and depraved men.'[7] Cotter did well during his time on the training ship and was highly thought of by Thurburn, who described him as a 'smart active lad' and a 'teetotaller.'[8] He was made a leading hand and awarded the ship's sail-making prize and two gold badges for good conduct. Ironically, on at least two occasions around the time Cotter was on the *Chichester*, visitors were highly impressed by the efficiency with which the trainee seamen tackled fire-fighting.[9]

After leaving *Chichester* on 24 March 1873, Cotter first shipped to Brazil and North Africa before joining the barque-rigged steamer *Tartar* for China and Australia. He quit the *Tartar* in Melbourne and in February 1874 signed articles on the sailing ship *Dallam Tower*, whose voyage from

London to Port Chalmers had, months earlier, been interrupted by storm damage sustained in the Southern Ocean. Pounded by a series of gales in June 1873, *Dallam Tower* lost all three masts and reached Melbourne only after an epic passage of 2000 miles under jury rig. Cotter cleared out from the partially refitted vessel when, after further alarms brought about by the Melbourne shipyard's inadequate repairs, *Dallam Tower* finally reached Port Chalmers on 6 March 1874. Six days later he was arrested for ship desertion and, on 20 March, sentenced in the Port Chalmers Police Court to four weeks' hard labour.[10] Cotter offered no defence to the charge and the records give no indication as to why he quit the ship. Most British seamen who deserted in New Zealand did so because of the good wages on offer, but this might not have been a factor for Cotter, since his stay in the country was short. After release from prison in April he made his way to Lyttelton, where he joined the Shaw, Savill & Co. iron barque *Hudson*. The *Hudson* sailed from Lyttelton on 14 May and arrived at Gravesend on 6 August. One month later Cotter, signed articles of employment for the *Cospatrick* as she lay in London's East India Docks.

As a *Cospatrick* survivor he was accorded celebrity status, albeit briefly. Victorians had a fascination with those who managed to cheat death, and fortunate survivors were treated as both curiosities and heroes. Cotter soon found himself featuring in a London music-hall show run by an impresario named Charles Williams. As the show was moved between venues, so great was the enthusiasm to see him that more than once the windows of his carriage were broken in the crush. His participation in survival cannibalism provided an added attraction and he was greeted with storms of cheering whenever he appeared on stage. 'I was brass bound in the company's uniform at that time,' he later said, 'and I dare say I was a very fine draw for the performance, though I did not realise it then.'[11]

In between stints at sea, Cotter had two periods of employment with London's Metropolitan Fire Brigade. He first joined the Brigade on 4 July 1878 and after preliminary training was assigned to the Clerkenwell Fire Engine Station as a fourth-class fireman in August. The contrast with his apparently exemplary behaviour on *Chichester* is striking – in October he was fined for 'using threatening and abusive language to his senior', and

Edward Cotter in 1911.
(*Lloyd's Weekly News*, 1911)

later in the month was brought before the Brigade Board on a charge of being 'drunk on duty and violently assaulting his senior'.[12] In an attempt to delay the inevitable he instituted legal proceeding against the board, but was dismissed at the end of November. He successfully negotiated re-appointment to the Brigade late in 1891, but only by giving false information regarding his date and place of birth.[13] Cotter often exhibited considerable flexibility when furnishing these particulars, but the bulk of evidence suggests he was born at Fermoy, Cork, on 1 May 1857.[14]

He was assigned to the Holborn fire engine station in March 1892, but was removed to the Scotland Yard station in May, and, hard on the heels of two serious offences against station discipline, to Islington in October. In December he married Jane Allan, aged 28, at St George's Church, Kensington, but was soon creating further difficulties for his employer. Severely reprimanded and briefly suspended for being drunk on duty in January 1893, he was fined for being absent without leave and missing an engine in June. In August he was suspended for being 'under the influence of drink while on duty & quarrelling and fighting with strangers'. Before a Brigade committee could be assembled to dismiss him, Cotter resigned to escape punishment. It was some time before the Brigade realised that the man they had been dealing with was the one who had caused so many problems 15 years earlier: 'The deception … not being discovered, unfortunately, until his resignation had been accepted,' recorded the exasperated chief station officer of the Islington Depot.[15]

At some time after 1893, *Chichester*'s shipping agent met Cotter in London and reported that he was boatswain on Shaw Savill's *Lady Jocelyn*. Presumably this was during the period – up until 1899 – when the old ship was in use as a floating refrigerated warehouse in the West India Docks. However, he continued to lead a roving life. According to his own statements he worked in the Australian outback, both as a goldminer and, at Farina, for the locomotive department of the South Australian Government. He was drawn to Canada's far north at the height of the Klondike gold rush, and spent two years on the Yukon River, panning for gold and transporting miners and supplies by stern-wheel paddle steamer.

In 1911 Cotter, now aged 54, was living in London at 81 Campden Street, Kensington (the three-storeyed terrace house still exists), where he gave an account of the *Cospatrick* disaster to *Lloyd's Weekly News*.[16] Any sense of loyalty toward McDonald had long since disappeared and he used the interview as an opportunity to accuse his former shipmate of stealing from the dead. 'He received the cash of every man who entered the boat and had any to give,' stated Cotter. Of the Cornish emigrant John Bunt, who had died in the boat, Cotter said: 'I saw nearly £200 taken out of his pocket. I told the Lord Mayor so at the time [that Bunt's friends enquired of his possessions at the Mansion House], but he declined to make any more bother about it.'

Cotter made other allegations. He claimed to have lied to the Board of Trade inquiry about the lamps carried on the *Cospatrick*. He had told the court that all the lamps were locked, but in 1911 said: 'there were any number of them without locks'. He particularly mentioned an old-fashioned lamp, which had two spouts with a loose piece of wick stuck in each. The lamp was kept on a shelf in the boatswain's locker, and because of the way the ship was rolling at the time the fire broke out, Cotter was in no doubt it would have toppled over. Of course, if it was the source of ignition it must have been left alight. William Symons, the boatswain and the man with the greatest access to the locker, was suggested as the culprit – for in Cotter's opinion 'Symons was a very careless man.'[17] Lewis and McDonald, the two men who might have refuted these charges, were by this time long dead. Cotter himself died of cardiac failure at his Campden Street house on 23 February 1941, at nearly 84 years of age.

Charles Henry McDonald (known as Henry) was born at Leith in 1845. He married Jane Richardson of Montrose on 21 December 1866 and obtained his mate's certificate at Dundee in January 1870. He was subsequently employed on various vessels in the Baltic trade, and from 1871 to 1874 was mate on *Zambeze*, *Lizzie Morrow*, *Ravensbourne*, and *Heath Park* to Demerara. This succession of voyages to the West Indies was punctuated by trips to Picton, New Zealand, on the emigrant ship *Zemindar* in 1872, and to New Brunswick on the barque *Neptune* in 1873. It was in January of this year that McDonald passed his examination for master at Dundee. In 1874 he and Jane maintained a home at 45 Castle Street, Montrose, close to the town centre.

At the time of his return to Montrose in 1875, McDonald was hoping for a shore appointment with Shaw, Savill & Co., and although this failed to eventuate, he never went to sea again. Notoriously, however, he has been credited with surviving two later shipwrecks. At least one maritime historian has him as second mate on the *Ben Venue* when the vessel was driven ashore during a gale at Timaru, New Zealand, in May 1881, and also has him on the *St Leonards*, at the time of her sinking off Start Point following a collision in September 1883.[18] Naturally both reports are erroneous.[19] '*Cospatrick*'s McDonald' was also said to have been second mate on the *St Leonards* during her 1873 voyage to New Zealand,[20] but has here been confused with a John McDonald, born at Stromness in 1841.

In February 1875, Henry McDonald was reunited with Captain William Jahnke when the *British Sceptre* arrived at Dundee with her cargo of jute. McDonald was, as might be expected, 'exceedingly happy to see his deliverer.'[21] Shortly after this meeting Shaw Savill marked their appreciation of Jahnke's humanity toward the *Cospatrick* survivors by presenting him with a suitably inscribed two-day chronometer.

In 1876 Henry and Jane McDonald were living in Dundee, and

McDonald was working as a manager for sewing machine manufacturer Kimball & Morton of 52 Reform Street. Despite giving up the sea he was unable to shake off the effects of his experiences in the lifeboat, and as the years passed the darker side of his character, hinted at by Archibald Forbes in his *Daily News* articles,[22] became more and more evident. From 1880 to 1885 McDonald was a publican and wine and spirit merchant at premises located at 1 Westport, Dundee, and he and Jane moved house several times during this period. His new occupation contributed to a rapid mental decline, and he was addicted to drink and 'in a state of melancholy' when admitted to the Dundee Royal Lunatic Asylum on 21 February 1885. Although in reasonable physical health, his behaviour was causing great concern and he was assessed as uncommunicative and 'outrageous and homicidal'.[23] He had become violent and abusive toward his friends and had threatened Jane's life. It appears that at the time of his committal McDonald had no desire to live; he obstinately refused to take food (a symptom almost certainly associated with events in *Cospatrick*'s starboard lifeboat) and asylum staff were reduced to force-feeding him with a stomach pump. Electro-convulsive therapy failed to improve his condition and on 2 April he was bound in a straitjacket and confined to bed. On the following day a fever set in and he grew steadily weaker.

Charles Henry McDonald died in the Dundee Royal Lunatic Asylum at 7.50 a.m. on 5 April 1885, aged 39. His death notice in the *Weekly News* (Dundee) of 11 April subtly reflects family anguish at the manner of his demise – it is the only one in which the place of death is not mentioned. Jane McDonald never remarried. She lived for a further 41 years and died in a Dundee poorhouse at the age of 78.

APPENDIX 1
LIFEBOAT OCCUPANTS FROM THE
WRECK OF THE *COSPATRICK*

Port lifeboat			Starboard lifeboat	
1	Charles Romaine	1st Mate	Henry McDonald	2nd Mate
2	Thomas Doughery	QM	Thomas Lewis	QM
3	Frank Bellifanti	AB	Robert Hamilton	AB
4	Alfred Nicolle	"	John McNeil (Scottie)	"
5	Thomas Turvey	"	Edward Cotter	OS
6	Charles Cunningham	"	Peter Cope	Baker
7	Harry Boscobie	"	William King	Cook
8	John Langdon	"	Edward Bickersteth	Passenger
9	Charles Hancock	"	Thomas Lewis	Emigrant
10	William Wood	OS	John Bunt	"
11	Alfred Dutton	Butcher	Robert Scott‡	"
12	Catherine Harvey	Emigrant	John McBride	"
13	William Harvey	"	Jeremiah Leuchan	"
14	Mary Shea	"	Thomas Bentley	"
15	John Marsh	"	Frederick Bentley	"
16	Caroline Marsh	"	John Anderson	"
17	Edward Whitehead	"	Tom Pascoe	"
18	Mary Whitehead	"	William Eagles	"
19	Infant Whitehead	"	Benjamin Reeves	"
20	Bartholomew Geary	"	Nicholas Birbeck§	"
21	Catherine Geary	"	boy Mahar‖	"
22	Arthur Colley	"	plus nine others¶	
23	Mahar*	"		
24	Robert Byron	"		
25	boy Wray	"		
26	David Lewis†	"		
plus six others				

QM Quartermaster
AB Able-bodied seaman
OS Ordinary seaman
*   Possibly James Mahar, aged 18.
†   Son of the emigrant Thomas Lewis.
‡   Scott was more than likely in this boat; a watch inscribed with his name was retrieved from one of the dead.
§   *The Scotsman* of 11 January 1875 reports his presence in McDonald's boat.
‖   Either Michael or Bartholomew Mahar.
¶   One of these was said to be 'a French soldier who died rather early'. This may have been Armand Henault; see *The Daily News* of 2 January 1875.

APPENDIX 2
VERSE INSPIRED BY THE *COSPATRICK*

The *Cospatrick* disaster was the source of inspiration for a popular song, 'Fearful Loss of Life at Sea!', written by Charles Fox and published in London at the end of 1874. It may well have been the topical song Edward Cotter later described himself as being 'worked into' while in association with music hall artist Charles Williams in 1875 (see reference 11, Chapter 8) At least two poems describing the catastrophe appeared in British provincial newspapers early in January 1875 and are reproduced below along with Fox's song. The novel *Where Lies the Land?*, written by James Sanders in 1976, is loosely based on the disaster. More recently, Ivan Jagni has used the theme in a composition for string quartet: *The Cospatrick Tragedy* (1992).

'Fearful Loss of Life at Sea!' by Charles Fox, December 1874

Air – 'Sailor's Grave'

Beneath the rude and restless waves
Many brave men have found their graves
Gallant ships when tempest toss'd,
Often go down with all hands lost;
But worse, far worse, than storm so dire,
Is to perish on the sea by fire;
An emigrant ship how sad to hear,
With four hundred souls is lost we fear.

Chorus
It was a fearful death to meet,
The burning ship beneath your feet,
Above four hundred souls so brave,
We fear have gone to a sailor's grave.

They had left behind them old England's ground,
To New Zealand they were bound,
The gallant ship whose fate's deplored,
Had nearly five hundred souls on board,
Men and women and a hardy crew,
One hundred and sixty children too:
Their ship was burnt upon the sea,
And launched them into eternity.

Midst scorching flames poor women fell,
Children at the breast as well,
Altho' this long voyage they had braved,
There's little hope that they were saved,
For fire and water both combined,
The raging flames and roaring wind,
Had siezed upon the doomed ship,
While fear stood trembling on each lip,

Far, far away from home and friends,
They met a sad and fearful end,
While travelling to a distant shore,
Their English homes they'd see no more,
In many a village and country town,
Weeping friends may now be found,
For those who lie beneath the sea,
Whose return can never be.

Many mothers we know were there,
Whose hearts were broken with despair;
Little children in great alarm,
Take refuge in their parent's arms;
A prayer was on each parting breath,
As old and young sank down to death,
To meet again in heaven we pray,
Where care and trouble pass away.

From rescued men who have returned,
Fearful tidings we have learn'd,
Of dreadful sufferings they went through,
Of horrid things compelled to do.
They had no food they had no drink,
At what they done perhaps you'll shrink;
God only knows what it must be,
In an open boat ten days at sea.

'The Burning of the *Cospatrick*', by T.B. Brindley,
published in the *Oxford Chronicle and Berks and Bucks Gazette* of 12 January 1875

Due south-west of the stormy Cape,
Behold a ship of comely shape
O'er ocean flying;
Trade winds had carried her along,
Whilst tropic breezes sweet had sung
To wavelets sighing.
Not from rude storm or ocean's strife
Suffered that beauteous 'thing of life',
which fast and frantic
Flew o'er the turgid water's foam
To find the emigrants a home
Beyond the Atlantic.

As midnight wrapped the world in gloom,
A sound like thunder's muffled boom,
And serpent's hissing
Broke on the silent hour of sleep;
Whilst lightnings leap into the deep,
The waters hissing
'Fire! fire!' – the dread alarm is given
Masts, by its red hot hands are riven
And seawards sweeping,
Whilst in and out among the shrouds,
And up into the crimson clouds
The flames are leaping.

O, God! What shall those heroes do,
Who with the pale but daring crew,
Rush through the burning
To man the boats, loved wives to save,
And snatch sweet children from the grave;
God's blessing earning
Ah! none may save those mothers wild,
Who now are pressing each loved child
To bosoms bleeding;
For all along the decks and shrouds
And midst the praying shrieking crowds
The demon's speeding.

Wildly they rush along the deck,
And plunge from off the burning wreck
Into the water;
Preferring much the sea to brave,
And die whilst battling the wave,
To fiery slaughter
Some swim and reach a waiting boat,
And others borne to safety float
Among the billow;
Four hundred sink beneath the foam,
And find in death, nor earthly home
Nor earthly pillow.

One boat alone remains to ride
The *British Sceptre* ship beside
And five men only
Are taken from that silent boat;
O, was such misery e'er afloat,
So dread and lonely.
Two died from trial overwrought,
Three others were to England brought
To tell the Story,
Which made all English bosoms creep,
And many a maiden wail and weep,
And parents hoary.

God gave the life he took away, –
All shall be clear on judgement day,
To man and nation,
Why some on fiery couches slept,
Why others were as dry leaves swept
To desolation
No matter if our spirits rest
In peace upon the saviours breast
All free from sorrow
Whether the summons comes today,
Or finds a fugitive delay
Until tomorrow.

Sufficient for frail man to know, –
Whatever winds of God may blow –
That all is right;
Trusting his wisdom power and love,
And seeking realms of bliss above,
Where all is light.

'The Ill-fated *Cospatrick*', by J.E. Styles,
published in the *Weekly Express* (Jersey) of 5 January 1875

How sad that tale from o'er the sea,
Just at the closing year;
What deep affliction it has wrought, –
What anguish and despair.
All England mourns the dreadful news,
Flashed through th' electric wire,
That a noble ship the *Cospatrick*,
Has been destroyed by fire.

In September last, the vessel sailed
For fair New Zealand's shore,
She had on board of emigrants
Four hundred souls and more;
Besides a crew of forty-one,
Of seamen kind and free;
Of whom, alas! – how sad to tell –
There now remain but three!

Elmslie was her commander's name,
And brave he proved to be,
For in the fight 'twixt death and life,
He jumped into the sea.
But ere he took that fatal leap
Into the briny wave,
He bid each one an effort make
Their precious lives to save.

Nay more he seized his darling wife,
And in the mighty foam,
He cast her from his brawny arms
To meet her last, long home.
Whilst overboard the doctor leaped,
Amidst death's piercing cry,
And in his arms he firmly bore
The captain's only boy.

A fearful scene it must have been,
On that momentous night;
Oh! may each one of us be spared
Such an appalling sight.
Grim death, alas! was busy there,
In every shape and form;
It was fire did the deadly work
And not the howling storm.

A terrible tale it is indeed;
It fills the mind with dread
To learn that those we knew so well
Are numbered with the dead;
Have found a tomb beneath the sea,
Amidst the surging foam,
Far from those they fondly loved,
Far far away from home.

The perils of the sea are great,
But greatest of them all,
Is that which in November last
The *Cospatrick* did befall.
Many who've read the narratives
From those now safe on land
Have heaved a sigh; – aye shed a tear
For that ill-fated band.

Poor hapless souls! ill-fated crew!
Oh! what a fearful sight
It must have been for each of them
On that eventful night.
Terror-stricken haggard, sad; –
All from the fire did flee; –
Husbands, mothers, sisters, brothers,
To perish in the sea.

God comfort those of friends bereft,
Of aged mother or sire,
Of brother, son or sister too,
By this appalling fire.
Give them strength to bear their grief,
Their dire affliction sore,
And may they meet in realms above
To part again no more.

APPENDIX 3
RECORD OF *COSPATRICK'S* 15 VOYAGES

Voyage	Comments
Master: Capt. G. Hodge. Arrived London from Moulmein 8 Aug. 1857.	Delivery voyage.
1. Master: Capt. C. Scott. Sailed from Portsmouth for the Cape (Table Bay) and Calcutta 7 Jan. 1858; arrived Calcutta 22 May.	Hired troopship carrying Ensign Keogh and 71 rank and file of the 80th Regt.; Ensigns Birch and Stace, one sergeant, one drummer and 49 rank and file of the 85th Regt.; Capt. Campbell, Ensign Gubbins and 50 rank and file of the 2nd Foot Regt.; Lieut. Bowen and 98 rank and file of the 6th Regt.; Ensigns Wigg, McKenzie and Poole, Asst. Surgeon Heydon and 68 rank and file of the 60th Royal Rifle Regt. (2nd Batt.); Capt. J.W. Burnes, Lieut. P.F. Shouldham, Ensigns A.H. Sharp and W.N. Piggott and 59 rank and file of the 73rd Regt.; Asst. Surgeon Herbert and 48 rank and file of the 45th Regt.; Asst. Surgeon L'Estrange of the Cape Mounted Rifles; Capt. Allan, Barrack Master of Cape Town. Thirty-one wives and 27 children accompanied the troops. Also on board were the Rev. Mr Quinn Mrs Quinn and a servant, which brought the total number of passengers to 532. Nine deaths occurred on the voyage.
1a. Master: Capt. C. Scott. Sailed from Calcutta 30 July 1858; arrived Gravesend 8 Dec.	Carrying passengers and a general cargo consisting of saltpetre, linseed, mustard seed, jute, spices and tea. Eight passengers were landed at Hastings on 5 Dec. One death occurred on the voyage.
2. Master: Capt. C. Scott. Sailed from Plymouth 28 Jan. 1859; arrived Bombay 3 June.	Under charter and carrying military detachments from the Royal Artillery and 91st Regt. (originating from the dismasted troopship *Bombay*) for the East Indies. The vessel almost immediately returned to Plymouth owing to severe SW gales and sailed again on 1 February. Two deaths occurred on the voyage.
2a. Master: Capt. C. Scott. Sailed from Bombay 2 Oct. 1859; arrived Gravesend 22 Feb. 1860.	Hired troopship carrying units of the Bengal Light Cavalry and Bengal Artillery. There were six deaths during the passage.

3. Master: Capt. C. Scott. Sailed from Gravesend 15 July 1860; arrived Kurrachee (Karachi) 29 Oct.

Hired troopship carrying four officers and 35 men of the 31st Regt.; one officer and 60 men of the 94th Regt.; three officers and 61 men of the 64th Regt.; five officers and 134 men of the 79th Highlanders, and three officers and 111 men of the 93rd Highlanders. One death occurred during the voyage.

3a. Master: Capt. C. Scott. Sailed from Bombay 9 Jan. 1861; arrived Gravesend 22 Apr.

Under charter to the Hon. Council of India and carrying a general cargo together with nearly 300 military invalids under the command of Maj. Carmichael of the 95th Regt.; also Capt. James (6th Regt.), Capt. Oliver (95th Regt.), Lieut. Sweeney (4th Dragoon Guards), Lieut. O'Dowd and Cornet Goldsmith (6th Dragoon Guards). Twelve deaths and one birth occurred during the voyage.

4. Master: Capt. C. Scott. Sailed from Gravesend 16 July 1861; arrived Bombay 11 Nov.

Under charter to the Hon. Council of India for the conveyance of reinforcements: two officers and 26 men of the 17th Lancers; Capt. Eccles, one other officer and 70 men of the 56th Regt.; one officer and 50 men of the 72nd Highlanders; 120 non-commissioned officers and men of the 4th King's Own Regt. under the command of Ensigns William. H.E. Kemp and Edgar M. Evans. The troops were accompanied by the 'usual proportion' of women and children. A general cargo included 130 cases of ale, and 50 cases of wine. Four deaths occurred during the voyage.

4a. Master: Capt. J.A. Elmslie. Sailed from Bombay 24 Jan. 1862; arrived Gravesend 22 May.

Hired troopship carrying Maj. Murray Capts. Bray and Dickenson, Lieut. Brymer, Ensigns Powis and Davis, Surgeon Mold, and 203 rank and file invalids of the 83rd and other regiments; also 8 insane soldiers, and 17 women and 40 children. On 8 Feb. *Cospatrick* rescued 12 men, two women and two boys from a vessel in distress in lat. 00.40 S. long. 76.29 E., and landed these people at St Helena on 5 April. There were six deaths during the passage.

5. Master: Capt. J.A. Elmslie. Sailed from Gravesend 18 Aug. 1862; arrived Bombay 5 Dec.

First voyage under the ownership of Smith, Fleming & Co. and carrying livestock including 6 pure-bred merino rams, 2 shorthorned cows and a bull, and 4 brood mares belonging to the vessel's owners. A general cargo was also being carried which included coal, industrial metals (copper, zinc, brass, iron, steel), cases of acid, bottled beer and spirit wine.

5a. Master: Capt. J.A. Elmslie.
Sailed from Kurrachee 1 Mar. 1863; arrived Portsmouth 27 June.

Hired troopship carrying 170 invalids and 106 time-expired men of the 7th, 71st, 79th, 81st, 93rd and 98th Regts., the 7th Dragoon Guards and the Royal Artillery, with the troops being accompanied by 20 women and 39 children. Also on board were: Capt. McDonald (79th Highlanders); Capt. Hamilton (98th Regt.), plus Mrs Hamilton, two children and servant; Lieut. Clay (79th); Lieut. Harrison (7th Fusiliers); Asst. Surgeon Cameron; Lieut. Nixon (Indian Navy), plus Mrs Nixon and three children; Mrs Maj. Campbell, plus three children and servant; and nine steerage passengers. Six deaths and three births occurred during the voyage.

6. Master: Capt. J.A. Elmslie.
Sailed from Gravesend on 27 Nov. 1863; arrived Bombay 15 Apr. 1864.

Together with the sailing vessels *Marian Moore, Tweed, Kirkham, Assaye* and the steamer *Amberwitch, Cospatrick* was chartered by the Indian Government to transport out and lay the 1864 Persian Gulf Telegraph Cable. The vessel was extensively modified for deep-sea cable-laying both at Woolwich and after arrival in Bombay. While under tow from *Amberwitch* the *Cospatrick* and the *Assaye* laid the final section of cable between Gwadar and Kurrachee.

6a. Master: Capt. J.A. Elmslie.
Sailed from Bombay 3 Feb. 1865; arrived Portsmouth 6 May.

Hired troopship carrying 121 invalids and 181 time-expired men from various regiments and 14 women and 23 children. Accompanying the troops were: Capt. Leishman (Royal Artillery), plus wife and 2 children; Staff-Surgeon T. Clark; Lieut. Hammond (4th Kings Own); Lieut. Bridges (103rd Foot); Lieut. Heathcote (106th Foot); Lieut. Robertson (6th Dragoon Guards). There were two deaths and one birth during the passage.

7. Master: Capt. J.A. Elmslie.
Sailed from Portsmouth on 25 July 1865; arrived Bombay 1 Nov.

Hired troopship carrying the left wing of the 26th Regt. (Cameronians), with Capts. C.R.B. Calcott, G.E.P. Trent, J. Armstrong, G.S. Hamilton, and T. Lawson; Lieuts. L. Cubitt and W.B. Burton; Ensigns L. Clark, G.H. Wilson, F.S. Alexander, J.B. MacFarlane and J.B. Clark; Asst. Surgeon J. Johnston; three officers wives; 348 non-commissioned officers and men; 34 soldiers' wives, and 46 children. Three deaths and one birth occurred during the voyage.

7a. Master: Capt. J.A. Elmslie.
Sailed from Bombay 23 Dec. 1865; arrived Gravesend 28 Mar. 1866.

Hired troopship carrying detachments of invalids and time-expired men from the Royal Artillery, Royal Engineers, the 1st Royals, the 10th, 44th and 56th Infantry; 72nd Highlanders; 102nd Royal Madras Fusiliers and the 108th Madras Infantry, amounting to 256 non-commissioned officers and men, 17 women and 9 children. The troops were under the command of Capt. Ogilvie (R.A.); Second-Capt. Monckton (R.A.); Lieut. Rooke (1st Royals); Cornet Collette (4th Dragoons); Quartermaster M'Gee (1st Royals); Lieut. Knox (R.A.) and Dr. Green (44th Regt.). Six deaths occurred during the voyage.

8. Master: Capt. J.A. Elmslie.
Sailed from Queenstown (now Cork) 12 July 1866; arrived Bombay about 27 Oct.

Hired troopship carrying the left wing of the 1st battalion 2nd Queens Royal Regt., with Maj. Richard Hill Rocke commanding; Capts. Edward Hawker Helyar and James Wharton Harrel; Lieuts. R.A. Crawford, Charles Davie and J.A. Scott; Ensigns Arthur Mudge, Frederick Adams, Bernard Arthur Beale, John Fergusson, Richard Salisbury Simpson and William Montgomery; Asst. Surgeon William Tomlinson, 343 non-commissioned officers and men, 40 women and 37 children. There were two births during the passage.

8a. Master: Capt. J.A. Elmslie.
Sailed from Kurrachee 29 Jan. 1867; arrived Portsmouth 8 May.

Hired troopship carrying 175 invalid soldiers from various regiments, 15 women and 38 children. The officers accompanying the troops were Capt. E.W. Cuming and Lieut. Fergusson (79th Highlanders); Lieuts. Walter and Colquhoun (42nd Royal Highlanders); and Staff Asst. Surgeon Walter John. Other passengers were: Mrs Cuming and two children; Dr Moorshead (R.A.) plus wife and one child; Quartermaster Hammond (108th Regt.) plus wife and three children; Mrs Robinson and two children; Mr Larcomb and Mr Peverill. Three deaths and two births occurred during the voyage.

9/9a. Master: Capt. A. Elmslie.
Sailed from Gravesend 11 Sept. 1867; arrived Sydney 14 Dec. Sailed from Sydney 27 Feb. 1868; arrived Gravesend 31 May.

On the outward voyage the vessel carried general cargo, livestock, and the following passengers: Bishop Sawyer plus wife, five children and servant, Dr Sawyer, Lord Bertrand Gordon, Miss Dampier, Miss Snell, Mr Compagnoni and wife, Mrs Hassard, Messrs Carpenter and Dampiere. One death occurred during the passage. On the homeward voyage the vessel carried a cargo of wool and the following passengers: Mr Evans plus wife, three children and servant, Dr Rowland, Miss Eastwood, Miss Carey, Messrs Greenhill, Masey and Farmer.

10. Master: Capt. A. Elmslie.
Sailed from Gravesend 3 Aug. 1868; arrived Kurrachee 27 Nov.

Under charter to the Hon. Council of India and conveying cavalry and artillery troops: 42 non-commissioned officers and men, five soldiers' wives and 17 children of the 5th (Royal Irish) Lancers; 40 men of all ranks, four women and two children of the 20th Hussars; 82 non-commissioned officers and gunners, five women and four children of the Royal Horse Artillery; four officers, 126 non-commissioned officers and gunners, 12 soldiers' wives and 13 children of the Royal Artillery. Officers embarked with the troops were: Capt. J.R. Rapee, Capt. J.R. Macleay and Lieut. E.W. Adams (R.A.), Capt. J. Chaffey (5th Lancers), Lieut. J.S. Black (11th Hussars) and Asst. Surgeon G.S. Davie (R.A.). Five births occurred during the voyage.

10a. Master: Capt. A. Elmslie.
Sailed from Madras 2 May 1869; arrived Gravesend 26 Sept.

On 14 Dec. 1868 the vessel arrived at Bombay from Kurrachee and cleared for Rangoon 22 Jan. 1869. She arrived at Galle under tow from the s.s. *Punjaub* on 2 Feb. and on the 8th sailed for Madras via Rangoon. The vessel arrived at Madras on 4 Mar.

11/11a. Master: Capt. A. Elmslie.
Sailed from Gravesend 10 Jan. 1870; arrived Bombay 22 Apr.

The vessel sailed from Bombay on 4 July 1870. She arrived at Havre on 22 Sept. and at Gravesend on 7 Nov.

12. Master: Capt. A. Elmslie.
Sailed from Gravesend 3 Dec. 1870; arrived Port Phillip Melbourne 11 Mar. 1871

443 Emigrants (names are available through the State Library of Victoria) were landed at Melbourne. They were in the charge of Frederick West MD, Surgeon Superintendent and Miss Cox, Matron. One death occurred during the passage.

12a. Master: Capt. A. Elmslie.
Sailed from Port Phillip for Colombo, Cocanada and London 16 Apr. 1871; arrived London 16 Nov.

Carrying cavalry mounts (55 horses), fodder, 12 cows and 532 tons of coal for the East Indies.

13/13a. Master: Capt. A. Elmslie.
Passed from the river (Thames) for Bombay 19 Jan. 1872; arrived Bombay 7 June.

On the outward voyage the vessel carried a general cargo which included 564 casks of beer, 148 casks of pale ale, spelter, copper sheet and yellow metal. The vessel sailed from Bombay for Tuticorin on 17 July and departed from Tuticorin on 24 Aug. Vessel arrived at Gravesend on 17 Dec. 1872.

14. Master: Capt. A. Elmslie.
Passed from the river (Thames) for Otago 21 Mar. 1873; arrived Port Chalmers, New Zealand 6 July.

Carrying passengers, livestock and general cargo (including explosives and railway plant for the New Zealand Government). Suffered storm damage when in lat. 45° 30′ S., long. 101° 00′ E. and landed 45 passengers in Otago. Among these were: Messrs Wood, Mitchell and Beard; Edward and Elizabeth Avard and one child; William and Mary McMillan and five children (while on board Mrs. McMillan gave birth to a son); Frederick and Eliza Page, George and Caroline Page and three children; Frederick and Eliza Tozer and three children; John Brown, Mary Fenwick, Emily Mill, Elizabeth Taylor, Hugh Campbell, Patrick Culkeen, Alfred Markham, Henry Roach, Thomas Broderick, Helen Campbell, Maria McPherson, Mary Calkeen, Margaret Deveny.

14a. Master: Capt. A. Elmslie.
Sailed from Port Chalmers 25 Aug. 1873; arrived Gravesend 26 June 1874.

Sailed in ballast for Newcastle, N.S.W. and loaded coal for Calcutta – arrived there on 8 Nov. and departed with 481 coolies (indentured labourers) for Cayenne (French West Indies) on 23 Dec. Loaded sugar and rum at Demerara (British West Indies) and sailed for London in May 1874. Twenty-two deaths and three births occurred on the passage between Calcutta and Cayenne.

15. Master: Capt. A. Elmslie.
Sailed from Gravesend 11 Sept. 1874 for Auckland, New Zealand.

Carrying a general cargo that included nearly 6000 gallons of spirits together with four passengers, 429 emigrants, a crew of 44, and the master's wife and small son. The vessel caught fire when in the South Atlantic, and sank on the afternoon of 19 Nov. 1874; three crew members survived.

* Compiled from Lloyd's List, the Naval and Military Intelligence columns of *The Times*, *Cableships and Submarine Cables*, K.R. Haigh, Adlard Coles, London 1968, *The India Times*, the *Bengal Hurkaru and India Gazette*, the *Argus* (Melbourne), the *Sydney Morning Herald*, the *Otago Daily Times*, and the Register of Births, Deaths and Marriages at Sea (BT 158).

APPENDIX 4
BIRTHS AND DEATHS DURING THE
COSPATRICK'S FIRST 14 VOYAGES

Deaths

Daughter of Sgt. Collins, 6 mths, measles, February 1858
Son of Pvt. Henton, 60th Rifles, 2 yrs, dysentery, 24/4/1858
James Dowling, 21 yrs, 60th Rifles, dysentery, 29/4/1858
Daughter of Gunr. Brown, 1 yr, dysentery, 29/4/1858
Son of Gndr. Morris, 80th Regt., 4 mths, measles, 2/5/1858
Pvt. Collins, 23 yrs, 60th Rifles, inflammation of brain, 13/5/1858
Pvt. Parker, 20 yrs, 6th Regt., inflammation of brain, 14/5/1858
Elizabeth Morris, 80th Regt., 25 yrs, gastritis, 14/5/1858
Pvt. Dakin, 22 yrs, 60th Rifles, inflammation of brain, 22/5/1858
Ensign F. A. Allan, 39 M.N.I., dysentery, 7/8/1858

Pvt. Joseph Sickles, 91st Regt., inflammation of lungs, 7/5/1859
Gnr. James Buttler, inflammation of lungs, 19/5/1859

Pvt. Seamus Banfield, 28 yrs, Bengal Light Cav., gen. debility, 18/1/1860
Pvt. Timothy Kelly, 30 yrs, Bengal Artillery, rheumatism and gen. debility, 21/1/1860
Pvt. James Pigler, 25 yrs, Bengal Light Cav., dysentery, 21/1/1860
Pvt. John Williams, 27 yrs, Bengal Artillery, inflammation of lungs, 31/1/1860
Pvt. Joseph Black, 22 yrs, Bengal Light Cav., dysentery, 17/2/1860
Pvt. William Dawes,, Bengal Artillery, chronic rheumatism, 22/2/1860
Alexander Ballance, 74th Highlanders, fell overboard, 17/9/1860

Samuel Leitch, 57th Regt., consumption, 22/1/1861
James Cannaway, 43 yrs, 57th Regt., dysentery, 25/1/1861
James Crocker (soldier), dysentery, 5/2/1861
Thomas Flanagan, 24 yrs, 57th Regt., dysentery, 14/4/1861
William Minton, 36 yrs, 56th Regt., gastric fever, 20/3/1861
Male Maldive Islander, gen. debility, 25/3/1861
Michael Walsh, 35 yrs, 83rd Regt., heart disease, 18/4/1861
John Burns, 4th Regt., pulmonary consumption, 19/4/1861
James Hopkins (soldier), chronic dysentery, 23/4/1861
John Malone (soldier), 24 yrs, secondary syphilis, 3/5/1861
John Murphy, 26 yrs, 56th Foot, inflammation of lung, 12/5/1861
Marg. Bedall, 2 yrs, soldier's child, Faber mesenterica, 15/5/1861
John Harold, 1½ yrs, soldier's child, convulsions, 10/8/1861
Ann Doherty, 3 yrs, soldier's child, Faber mesenterica, 17/8/1861
Ellen Mary Smith, 13 mths, soldier's child, gen. debility, 27/8/1861
Henry Ponter, 56th Regt., 20/9/1861

Wm. Corrigan, 83rd Regt., gen. debility, 24/1/1862
David Agnes, 95th Regt., disease of liver, 7/2/1862
Jeremiah Chivers, 56th Regt., dysentery, 7/2/1862
George Avery (soldier), disease of liver, March 1862
M. Shaughnessy, 83rd Regt., sec. syphilis, 7/3/1862
Stephen Coorley, 86th Regt., morb. cor anasarca, 17/3/1862

P. Sweeney (soldier), dysentery, 13/3/1863
Thos. Hartgroves, 2 yrs, fever, 25/3/1863
C. Smith (soldier), dysentery, 6/4/1863
J. Geddes, 9 yrs, fever, 9/4/1863
R. Ord (soldier), dysentery, 31/5/1863
Escott (soldier), dysentery, 27/6/1863

Ronald McDonald, Royal Artillery, consumption, 16/4/1865
Henry Simpson, liver, 16/4/1865
John Bell, 5 mths, diarrhoea, 7/8/1865
Marg. Maguire, 2 yrs, convulsions, 30/9/1865
E.C. Hilditch, 2 mths, whooping cough, 12/10/1865

John Edwards (soldier), 30 yrs, dysentery, 6/1/1866
Wm. Braithwaite (soldier), 28 yrs, dysentery, 21/1/1866
James Teddy (soldier), 29 yrs, bubo., 22/1/1866
John Connor (soldier), 35 yrs, phthisis, 6/2/1866
Joseph Cole (soldier), 30 yrs, dysentery, 23/2/1866
James Evine (soldier), 48 yrs, dysentery, 20/3/1866

Henry Warneke (soldier), 25 yrs, consumption, 21/2/1867
W. Henry, 30 yrs, consumption, 28/2/1867
C. Sheldon, 30 yrs, consumption, 4/3/1867
I.C. Shean, 3 mths, pneumonia, 17/10/1867

June Edwards, 68 yrs, bronchitis, 24/12/1870

Coolies: 11 male and 11 female deaths, various causes, 25/12/1873 to
26/3/1874

Births

To: Sgt. John and Elizabeth White, female child, 6/2/1861

McClellan (soldier's wife), gender not known, 31/3/1863
Jarvis (soldier's wife), gender not known, 5/6/1863
Geddes (soldier's wife), gender not known, 26/6/1863

A.J. and A.G. Elmslie, male child (Archibald G.), 22/3/1865
Robert and Mary Hilditch, female child (Elizabeth Cospatrick), 12/8/1865

John and Catherine Shean, male child, 12/7/1866
Pvt. and B. Coupleditch, male child, 15/9/1866

Mr and Mrs McKnight, male child, 30/1/1867
Sgt. and Mrs Grey, male child, 6/4/1867

Edmund and Mary Ann Newman, male child (Edmund Cospatrick), 18/8/1868
John and Bridget Conway, gender not known, 8/9/1868
Mr and Mrs Murray, female child, 20/9/1868
Walter and Susannah Hinlay, gender not known, 8/10/1868
William and Emma Hull, gender not known, 31/10/1868

William and Mary Jane McMillan, male child, 24/6/1873
Various coolies, one male and two female children, between 24/12/1873 and 21/3/1874

* These records (contained in the Register of Births, Deaths and Marriages at Sea, BT 158) are derived from entries in the ship's log and are probably incomplete.

APPENDIX 5
REGISTER OF ACCOUNTS OF WAGES FOR
COSPATRICK'S DECEASED SEAMEN

Name*	Rating	Age	Amount owing		
			£	s	d
Romaine, Charles	1st Mate	35	10	15	0
Jones, Brasher	3rd Mate	20	5	3	0
Cadle, Dr. James. F.	Surgeon	32	0	0	10
Fidler, John L.	Carpenter	29	8	17	8
Symons, William	Bosun	36	6	11	6
Smith, John	Sailmaker	53	1	4	10
Wakefield, Thomas	Steward	32	in debt		
Wilkins, John	Cook	43	0	11	6
Belfonti, Frank (Bellifanti)	AB	33	3	18	2
Turvey, Thomas	"	20	3	18	2
Langdon, John H.	"	45	3	18	2
Frank, Henry	"	32	3	18	2
Hamilton, Robert	"	20	3	18	2
Peach, Charles	"	27	3	18	2
Hancock, Charles	"	43	3	18	2
Paren, Matthew	"	28	3	18	2
Mills, George	"	21	3	18	2
Gunnighe, Chas. (Cunningham)	"	36	3	18	2
Doogery, Thos. (Doughery)	"	27	3	18	2
Demache, Michael	"	—	3	18	2
McNeill, John	"	19	3	18	2
Walsh, John	"	19	3	18	2
Smith, Charles	"	24	0	16	6
Crompton, Henry	"	34	2	16	6
Nicolle, Alfred E.	"	24	0	16	6
Ruskin, Harry (Boscobie)	"	27	3	18	2
Pillow, Thomas†	"	20	1	1	6
Attwell, Hubert	OS	14	1	14	0
Wood, James (Wood, William James)	"	17	1	11	6
Lockett, George	"	18	1	11	6
Bennett, Alfred‡	Engine driver	24	7	11	6
Dutton, Alfred	Butcher	25	4	18	2
Cope, Peter	Baker	19	2	4	10
King, William	Cook	47	4	18	2
Hopkins, Peter	Cook	41	4	18	2
Godlonton, Robert (Godliaton)	Steward	19	4	18	2
Lopez, Alfred	Boy	16	1	11	6

Lane, William Harry	Apprentice	15	in debt		
Barrow, Arthur Frederick	"	17	in debt		
Harrison, Corey Crawford	"	20	4	7	10

AB Able-bodied seaman

OS Ordinary seaman

*   More probable or correct name given in parentheses.

†   Was an ordinary seaman not an AB.

‡   Responsible for operating the ship's distillation plant.

Appendix 6

Passenger List for the *Cospatrick's* 15th Voyage

Steerage Passengers

Bickersteth Edward 22
Mason   G. 35
Nelson   William 25
Simister   William 21

Assisted Emigrant Families*

Surname	Name	Age	Origin	Occupation
Archibald	George	24	Middlesex	Gen. labourer
	Anna Marie	23		
Bailey	Reuben	23	Worcestershire	Shepherd
	Emma	23		
	Jane E.	2		
	Emma	Infant		
Bentley	Thomas	37	Lancashire	Gen. labourer
	Frances	36		
	Frederick A.	11		
	Harriet	8		
	Ernest S.	4		
Berriman	Caleb	37	Gloucestershire	Gardener
	Mary A.	32		
Beswetherick	John Henry	22	Cornwall	Farm servant
	Emma	27		
	Thomas Warne†	11		
	Alfred Warne†	7		
Blincow	John	29	Oxfordshire	Labourer
	Emma	30		
	Naomi	6		
	Elizabeth	10 mths		
Blott	Frederick	26	Middlesex	Carpenter
	Sophia	25		
Bradley	Joseph	30	Cheshire	Labourer
	Mary	30		
	Frederick	9		
	Mary Elizabeth	8		
	Sarah	5		
Brown	George	35	Essex	Farm labourer
	Emma	34		
	Alfred	10		

Surname	Name	Age	Origin	Occupation
	John	6		
Bunt	John	25	Cornwall	Miner
	Sarah	25		
Byron	Robert	34	Ayr	Navvy/Labourer
	Jane	32		
	Robert	9		
	Marion	6		
	John	18 mths		
Caldwell	Robert	29	Ayr	Rope maker
	Jessie	27		
	Hugh	4		
	Robert	1		
Campbell	Arthur	26	Antrim	Farm labourer
	Emma J.	28		
	William James	1		
Carroll	Edmond	36	Tipperary	Farm labourer
	Ann	35		
	Mary	8		
	Edward	5		
Chapman	Joseph M.	37	Kent	Carpenter
	Agnes	38		
	Joseph Andrew	11		
	Margaret	10		
	Maud	2		
Charter	George	31	Cambridge	Labourer
	Jane	33		
	George	4		
	Mary J.	1		
Coleman	John	26	Waterford	Farm labourer
	Mary	26		
Cousins	William‡	20	Down	Labourer
	Mary‡	22		
Crossley	George	30	Derbyshire	Farm labourer
	Amelia	30		
	Amer	2		
Dalton	Charles‡	50	Antrim	Constable
	Ellen‡	49		
Davis	John	27	Warwickshire	Carpenter/Joiner
	Ann	25		
Doyle	John	24	Kilkenny	Shepherd
	Eliza	23		
Farrell	James	35	Galway	Labourer
	Bridget	36		

Surname	Name	Age	Origin	Occupation
	Patrick	6		
	Michael	5		
	Bridget	3		
	John	6 mths		
Fitzgerald	Robert	33	Cork	Ag. labourer
	Mary A.	34		
	William	8		
	Ann M.	6		
	Robert	4		
	Elizabeth	2		
Foulgham	Richard	25	Nottinghamshire	Ag. labourer
	Eliza	22		
	Richard	9 mths		
Gale	Edward	26	Jersey	Tailor
	Annie	26		
Geary	Bartholomew	24	Cork	Farm labourer
	Catherine	25		
Hall	Thomas	28	Cornwall	Labourer
	Mary A.	31		
Hall	John	38	Herts	Labourer
	Elizabeth	38		
Harrison	William H.	25	Gloucestershire	Mason
	Selina	24		
	Emma	1		
Hedges	Henry W.	30	Oxfordshire	Farm labourer
	Mary	30		
	William	3		
	Charles	18 mths		
	George	4 mths		
Hedges	Richard	55	Oxfordshire	Labourer
	Sarah	55		
Hedges	John	24	Middlesex	Labourer
	Sarah	23		
Hefferman	Cornelius	25	Gloucestershire	Navvy
	Mary A.	30		
	Jane	6		
	Margaret	5		
	Arthur	3		
	Walter	3 mths		
Henault	Armand	44	Normandy	Carpenter
	Margaret	44		
Henderson	Andrew	21	Donegal	Constable
	Jane	20		

Surname	Name	Age	Origin	Occupation
Hogan	James	28	Queens County	Labourer
	Maria	28		
	Denis	3		
Holburn	William	30	Wiltshire	Labourer
(or Holbourne)	Mary	31		
	Arthur	1		
Hotton	George	28	Gloucestershire	Ag. labourer
	Ellen	27		
Irvins	James	36	Gloucestershire	Carpenter
	Hannah	38		
	Thomas Henry	10		
	Edith M.	6		
	Ernest L.	2		
Jacobs	John	47	Cornwall	Labourer
(or Jacob)	Mary	43		
	Emma	11		
Jones	George	49	Antrim	Labourer
	Bridget	44		
Jones	Philip	27	Glamorganshire	Navvy
	Sarah	25		
	Sarah A.	3		
	Mary	1		
Jones	Thomas	30	Warwickshire	Ag. labourer
	Ann	38		
Keating	Charles	43	Kerry	Gardener
	Mary	35		
	Mary	2		
Key	Henry Charles	35	Middlesex	Servant
	Selina	30		
	Sophia Jane	10		
King	William	25	Somersetshire	Shoemaker
	Mary A.	25		
Le Geyt	Abraham Joshua	23	Jersey	Farm labourer
	Elizabeth	22		
	Abraham	2		
Lee	William	32	Warwickshire	Carpenter
	Emma	29		
	Emily	7		
	Anne	5		
	James	2		
	William	5 mths		
Lewis	Thomas	40	Montgomeryshire	Cowman
	Maria	37		

Surname	Name	Age	Origin	Occupation
	David	11		
	Jane	2		
Mahar	John	41	Tipperary	Ag. labourer
	Mary	36		
	Margaret	9		
	Mary	7		
	Anne	5		
	Matthew	2		
Marsh	John E.	30	Warwickshire	Farm bailiff
	Caroline	33		
Meares	William	27		
(or Mearns)	Annie	26		
	John	6		
	James	4		
	William	2		
Mutton	William	25	Cornwall	Miner
	Mary	23		
	John	Infant		
Novell	George	44	Surrey	Farm labourer
	Sarah	41		
	Alfred	11		
	Arthur	8		
	Annie	3		
Orchard	Edward	38	Wiltshire	Farm labourer
	Louisa	23		
	Elizabeth	3		
	James	1		
Pearce	James H.	25	Cornwall	Farm labourer
	Harriet	27		
	Harriet	4		
	John S.	3		
	Martha	1		
Pearce	John	25	Derry	Farm servant
	Charlotte	20		
Reeves	Benjamin	26	Somersetshire	Labourer
	(or Reuben)			
	Eleanor	20		
Reilly	John	42	Dublin	Gardener
	Grace P.	31		
	Mary H.	4		
	Margaret	1		
Reilly	Patrick	44	Cavan	Farm labourer
	Margaret	28		

Surname	Name	Age	Origin	Occupation
	Mary E.	6		
	Florence	4		
	Annie	3		
	Catherine S.	10 mths		
Riordan	Jeremiah	34	Kerry	Farm labourer
	Elizabeth	32		
	Elizabeth	10		
	Michael	7		
	Thomas	4		
	Jerry	1		
Scarff	John	39	Larnarkshire	Mason's labourer
	Isabella	38		
	John	10		
Scott	Robert	22	Ayr	Labourer
	Ellen	19		
Sheward	Henry	34	Worcestershire	Ag. labourer
	Charlotte	39		
	Augusta	9		
	Charlotte	4		
Shore	Richard	25	Worcestershire	Carpenter
	Mary E.	20		
	Mary A.	2		
	Richard B.	1		
Shorthouse	Alexander	27	Larnarkshire	Labourer
(or Shorthorn)	Elizabeth	23		
Stallard	Thomas	45	Gloucestershire	Farm labourer
	Mary	32		
	George	9		
	Alice	7		
	Elizabeth	5		
	Emma	3 wks		
Thomson	John‡	38	Argyle	Joiner
	Barbara‡	35		
	Euphemia‡	7		
	Lachlan‡	5		
	John‡	3		
	Sarah‡	1		
Towille	James	28	Devonshire	Labourer
(or Towell)	Esther	27		
	Esther	2		
	Edwin	3 mths		
Townsend	Henry	60	Oxfordshire	Labourer
	Ann	55		

Surname	Name	Age	Origin	Occupation
Trevena	William	52	Cornwall	Farm labourer
	Jane	44		Servant
	Eliza	9		
	Francis	7		
	Richard	5		
Turner	George B.	22	Nottinghamshire	Blacksmith
	Maria	23		
	Florence A.	3		
Turner	John	34	Herefordshire	Labourer
	Julia	32		
	Charles	10		
	Elizabeth	8		
	William	6		
	Alice	10 mths		
Vincer	Edward Thomas	35	Hampshire	Cook
(or Vancer)	Caroline	26		
Wallis	Robert	36	Cornwall	Farm labourer
	Sarah H.	19		
Walters	William	31	Gloucestershire	Labourer
(or Waites)	Elizabeth	29		
	Mary	5		
	Charles	3		
	Alice	9 mths		
Welch	Frederick	21	Jersey	Ag. labourer
	Mary	21		
Whitehead	Edward	30	Warwickshire	Butcher
	Mary	30		
Whyte	William‡	27	Renfrew	Farm labourer
	Isabella‡	27		
	William‡	2		
	Elizabeth‡	8 mths		
Williams	John	34	Herefordshire	Labourer
	Mary A.	33		
	Mary A.	10		
	Emily	7		
	Charles	5		
	Ellen	6 mths		
Wray	William	38	Down	Farm labourer
	Mary	35		
	Hugh	10		
	Daniel	8		
	Kitty	6		
	Thomas	3		
	John	9 mths		

Assisted Emigrants Single Men

Surname	Name	Age	Origin	Occupation
Anderson	John	28	Lanarkshire	Ag. labourer
Bentley	John. J.	16	Lancashire	Carpenter
Birbeck	Nicholas J.	25	Yorkshire	Engineer
	John A.H.	21		Farmer
Bishop	Henry	19	Somersetshire	Carpenter
Bright	Joseph H.	18	Galway	
Brown	Thomas	13	Essex	
Calvert	John	21	Middlesex	Joiner
Clifton	Samuel	30	Oxfordshire	Ag. labourer
Colley	Arthur	23	Worcestershire	Gardener
Connell	Patrick	19	Kerry	Carpenter
Connor	James	20	Kerry	Farm labourer
Cook	Harry	20	Surrey	Carpenter
Duffield	William	24	Sussex	Coachman
Eagles	William	22	Gloucestershire	Labourer
Easton	John	18	Lanarkshire	Labourer
Flood	Denis	21	Lancashire	Ag. labourer
Foulgham	John	63	Nottinghamshire	Ag. labourer
	Willam	27		Ag. labourer
Gibson	Fred William	20	Middlesex	Coachman
Gilmer	George	21	Armagh	Farm labourer
Goodere	William	20	Worcestershire	Carpenter
Graham	Alexander	21	Renfrew	Navvy
Hammond	John	29	Nottinghamshire	Shepherd
Harvey	William	24	Donegal	Boot and shoemaker
Heath	Henry	21	Westmeath	Farm labourer
Hedges	Thomas	21	Oxfordshire	Labourer
	Charles	15		Labourer
Henault	Gustave	19	Normandy	Carpenter
	Theophile	15		Bronze worker
Hewitt	William Robert	22	Middlesex	Wheelwright
Hutchinson	James	22	Armagh	Farm labourer
Isaacs	David	25	Glamorganshire	Ag. labourer
Ivins	William James	13	Gloucestershire	Labourer
Jacobs	John	21	Cornwall	Miner
	Thomas	19		Smith
	Joseph	17		Carter
	Simon	15		Carter
Jones	David	22	Glamorganshire	Ag. labourer
Keating	Thomas	14	Kerry	

Surname	Name	Age	Origin	Occupation
Kerswell	George	28	Devonshire	Bricklayer
Lee	Thomas P.	19	Cork	Flourmill hand
Leuchan	Jeremiah	24	Cork	Ag. labourer
Lewis	William	17	Montgomeryshire	Cowman
	Thomas	15		
Livingstone	Robert	24	Lanarkshire	Labourer
	Duncan (John)	16		Labourer
	William	14		Tailor
Lloyd	Joseph	17	Hertfordshire	Labourer
Lockett	John	23		
Mack	Henry	25	Down	Ag. labourer
Mackinnon	John	22	Buteshire	Farm labourer
Mahar	James	18	Tipperary	Farm labourer
	John	17		
	Michael	13		
	Bartholomew	12		
McBean	James	21	Nairnshire	Gardener
McBride	John	27	Devonshire	Farm labourer
McLure	George	24	Antrim	Labourer
McFarland	James	24	Lanarkshire	Ag. labourer
McMechan	Robert	26	Antrim	Painter
McQuillin	Michael‡	22	Cavan	Labourer
Monat	James	17	Shetland	Ag. labourer
Muchensturn	Antoine	23	Strasburg	Gardener
Murphy	John	29	Waterford	Farmer
Nippin	Thomas	29	Northamptonshire	Ag. labourer
Novell	George	16	Surrey	Labourer
	Frederick	14		
Pascoe	Thomas	25	Cornwall	Farm labourer
Peacock	Alfred	21	Staffordshire	Carpenter
Prenter	Thomas	38	Cornwall	Farm labourer
Riordan	Timothy	14	Kerry	
Schwartze	Carlo‡	27	Switzerland	Farm labourer
Shaw	William	22	Down	Labourer
Shea	Michael	23	Kerry	Ag. labourer
Stapleton	Thomas	22	Norfolk	Blacksmith
Tagney	Howard	30		
Torrance	John	24	Lanarkshire	Labourer
Trevena	Samuel	22	Cornwall	Farm labourer
	Matthew	20		Farm labourer
	Charles	17		Farm labourer
	James	14		Farm labourer
	Joseph	12		

Surname	Name	Age	Origin	Occupation
Trewhella	William Thomas	21	Cornwall	Farm labourer
Turner	John	14	Herefordshire	Labourer
	James	12		
Vingoe (or Kingoe)	Henry. H.	28	Cornwall	Labourer
Warne	William	19	Cornwall	Farm labourer
Welch	Stephen	18	Jersey	Ag. labourer
White	George	21	Cork	Flourmill hand
Whyte	Robert S.‡	25	Renfrew	Engineer
(or Wayte)	Andrew‡	19	Renfrew	Joiner
Wray	William	18	Down	Farm labourer
	James	16		Farm labourer
	Frank	13		Farm labourer
Wurtze	Charles	22	Strasburg	Ag. labourer

Assisted Emigrants Single Women

Surname	Name	Age	Origin	Occupation
Burridge	Anne	27	Middlesex	Laundress
Byron	Mary	12	Ayr	
Campbell	Eliza	21	Armagh	Servant
Carroll	Johanna	16	Tipperary	Servant
	Margaret	13		
Dalton	Ellen	17	Antrim	Servant
Darvill	Maria	16	Berkshire	Housemaid
Doughton	Emily	17	Argyle	Servant
Edmonds	Elizabeth	21	Berkshire	Domestic servant
	Charlotte	18		Domestic servant
Foulgham	Mary	25	Nottinghamshire	Housemaid
	Harriet	24		Gen. servant
Hargrave	Ellen	22	Cornwall	Domestic servant
Harvey	Catherine	18	Donegal	Servant
Hefferman	Clara	12	Gloucestershire	
Henault	Isabella	14	Normandy	
Kirby (or Kelly)	Margaret	29	Waterford	Cook
Le Blond	Maria	19	Jersey	
Lewis	Alice	14	Montgomeryshire	
Mahar	Ellen	15	Tipperary	Servant
McCoy	Elizabeth	22	Antrim	Housemaid
McQueen	Margaret	21	Lanarkshire	Gen. servant

Surname	Name	Age	Origin	Occupation
Prenter (or Prember)	Susannah	26	Cornwall	Gen. Servant
Pritchard	Ellen	19	Herefordshire	Servant
Proctor	Amelia	30	Middlesex	Gen. servant
Pursey	Elizabeth	26	Somersetshire	Parlour maid
Quinn	Elizabeth	28	Warwickshire	Servant
Rickard	Ellen M.	23	Cornwall	Gen. servant
Riordan	Mary	12	Kerry	
Scarff	Margaret	19	Lanarkshire	Servant
	Jane	16		Servant
Shea	Mary	27	Kerry	Housemaid
Smith	Isabel	26	Kent	Nurse
Tangney	Honoria	33		Cook
Trevena	Susan	19	Cornwall	Servant
Trollope	Elizabeth	18	Wiltshire	Domestic
Weaver	Eliza	28		
Welch	Charlotte§	53	Jersey	Dressmaker
Whyte	Mary‡	58	Renfrew	Housekeeper
(or Wayte)	Jeanie (Jane)‡	32	Renfrew	Cook
Williams	Amelia	24	Middlesex	Kitchen maid
Wood	Mary††	33	Lanarkshire	Dressmaker
	John‖	3		
Wray	Mary	14	Down	

*   Children of 12 years of age and over are listed as single men or women.

†   Travelling with the Beswethericks.

‡   'Colonial nominated' emigrant (i.e. an emigrant to whom friends or family in New Zealand had given a guarantee of employment).

§   Matron for the single women.

‖   Male child travelling with his unattached mother.

The list comprises 82 married couples, 100 single men, 43 single women and 126 children and infants – a total of 433 passengers. There is no certainty as to the exact number; passenger lists published in British and New Zealand newspapers contain many inaccuracies, and even the official record (The Register of Births, Deaths and Marriages at Sea, BT 158) has duplicate entries (Johanna and Margaret Carroll, for example) and notable omissions.

NOTES

CHAPTER 1

1 *Tower Hamlets Independent*, 9 May 1874.
2 *The Times*, 11 July 1874.
3 See 1 above.
4 *Register of Accounts of Wages and Effects of Deceased Seamen*, File BT 153, National Archives, Kew, London.
5 The attitude of *Euxine*'s crew toward Murdoch greatly impressed St Helena's Shipping Master, Robert Noble: 'never before have I seen a crew on being discharged behave so respectfully toward a Master as this one has done; all bear testimony that it is owing to his coolness, self-possession and decision at the time of danger that as enabled them to make the land in safety.' Letter to the Assistant Secretary of the Marine Department of the Board of Trade, 21 August 1874. File MT 9/101, National Archives, Kew, London.
6 Affidavit of James Archer, given before the Hon. W.T. Fraser of the British Consulate in Batavia, on 6 November 1874. File MT 9/101, National Archives, Kew, London
7 Affidavit of August Müller, given before the Hon. W.T. Fraser of the British Consulate in Batavia, on 6 November 1874. File MT 9/101, National Archives, Kew, London
8 See 6 above.
9 See 7 above.
10 The agreement between depositions is not surprising considering how much was at stake.
11 *The Straits Times*, 13 November 1874.
12 *The Times*, 29 December 1874.
13 File MT 9/101, M 17,478, 1874. National Archives, Kew, London.
14 A.W.B. Simpson has elegantly described the intricacies of the case in *Cannibalism and the Common Law, A Victorian Yachting Tragedy*, Hambledon Press, London, 1994.

CHAPTER 2

1 W. Wood, *Survivor's Tales of Famous Shipwrecks*, Bles, London, 1932.
2 B. Lubbock, *The Blackwall Frigates*, 2nd edition, Brown, Son and Fergusson, Glasgow, 1950.
3 F.V. Smythe, 'Some Notes Relating to Dunbar Wharf, Limehouse and its Associations', 1935. National Maritime Museum, Greenwich.
4 *The Times*, 7 March 1862.
5 K.R. Haigh, *Cableships and Submarine Cables*, Adlard Coles, London, 1968; see also C. Bright, *Submarine Telegraphs*, Crosby, Lockwood & Son, London, 1898.
6 D. Savill, *Sail to New Zealand*, Robert Hale, London, 1986.
7 *Ibid*.
8 *Otago Daily Times*, 7 July 1873.
9 See 1 above.
10 Two members of crew deserted during *Cospatrick*'s visit to the island.
11 Fearon was later left to languish in a Demerara jail, see 12 below.
12 Official log book of the *Cospatrick*, 19 March 1873 to 26 June 1874. Maritime History Archive, Memorial University of Newfoundland.
13 *Ibid*.
14 The *Cornish Telegraph*, 6 January 1875.
15 British Sessional Papers (House of Commons), E.L. Erickson (ed.), XLIV.571, 1875.

16   Eleven seamen were taken on as replacements. The vessel's original complement of 35 changed drastically over the course of the voyage. What with desertion, discharge by mutual consent, promotion, engagement and re-engagement no fewer than 90 names were entered in the ship's articles, see 12 above.

17   McDonald left the *Heath Park* in Georgetown three weeks before joining the *Cospatrick*. (*Heath Park* foundered in the Atlantic in 1876). His father was a sugar planter in Demerara, and presumably it was the family connection that accounted for Henry's presence in the West Indies. The older McDonald had earlier been an iron-founder in Leith, Scotland and Henry (whose given name was Charles Henry McDonald, but who preferred to be called by his second name) was born in Leith in 1845. Another son, Osmond McDonald, born at Georgetown in 1851, subsequently lived in Glasgow and Edinburgh.

18   *Cospatrick* Report of Survey, File MT 9/99. National Archives, Kew, London.

CHAPTER 3

1   Evidence given before the 1885 *Royal Commission on Loss of Life at Sea* by Thomas Gray, Assistant Secretary of the Marine Department of the Board of Trade.

2   These vessels were lost at sea, rather than on inland waterways; see notes to the table on page 31.

3   *The Times*, 1 March 1887.

4   *The Times*, 16 March and 7 August 1846.

5   Seaton appears to have been gazetted Lieutenant Colonel before his death was known.

6   *The Times*, 8 April 1852.

7   *The Times*, 9 April 1852.

8   Fifty years later the principle was enshrined in Kipling's poem *Soldiers and Sailors Too*: 'But to stand an' be still in the Birken'ead Drill is a damn tough bullet to chew.'

9   W.S. Lindsay, *History Of Merchant Shipping and Ancient Commerce*, Vol. 3, Sampson, Low, Marston, Low and Searle, London, 1876.

10   Quoted in *The Times*, 30 January 1854.

11   *The Times*, 25 January 1854.

12   *Ibid.*

13   *Buenos Ayres Standard*; reported in *The Times*, 2 February 1872.

14   'Cubical capacity' was defined as the product of length by maximum breadth by depth amidships. An alternative formula: 0.6 by length by maximum breadth by depth amidships gave a better indication of a boat's internal volume, with one place in the boat being assigned for every 10 cubic feet of 'internal volume'.

15   To the point of being jettisoned if a boat's survival required lightening of its load. The most notorious example occurred in April 1841 when the American vessel *William Brown* was abandoned off Newfoundland after striking an ice floe. Bound for Philadelphia from Liverpool, the *William Brown* was carrying a crew of 17 and 65 passengers, the majority of whom were Irish and Scots emigrants. Owing to an insufficiency of boats, about 30 passengers were left on the vessel when she sank. Of the two boats that got away the longboat contained 41 or 42 people (nine of whom were seamen) and the jolly boat nine people (eight of whom were seamen). It was apparent from the outset that the longboat was not only greatly overloaded, but holed and leaking badly. The jolly boat, however, sailed off, leaving the longboat to its fate. Soon afterward, the longboat's sailors began to reduce its load by throwing passengers into the icy water. Of the 14 people jettisoned during the night of 20 April 12 were male passengers and two were women. The latter would

most likely have been spared had they not protested as their brother was being put over the side. Shortly after dawn on the 21st the sailors discovered two male passengers hiding behind the skirts of women. They were also thrown overboard, although the women shielding them were not harmed. Probably no more than one hour after the last of the passengers had been put over the side the longboat was sighted by an American ship, the *Crescent*, and the survivors were taken on board.

16 *The Times*, 8 June 1861.

17 G.H. Peters, *The Plimsoll Line, The Story of Samuel Plimsoll*, Barry Rose, Chichester, 1975.

18 However, it was not until 1890 that the position of 'Plimsoll's Line' was required to be fixed by marine survey.

19 See 1 above

20 See comments in *The Times*, 3 April 1873.

21 *The Times*, 19 April 1873

22 The *New York Herald*, 3 April 1873.

23 *Ibid.*

24 *The Times*, 17 April 1873.

25 A.F. Kynaston, *Casualties Afloat with Practical Suggestions for their Prevention and Remedy*, Trewlawney Saunders, London, 1846.

26 C. Clifford, *How to Lower Ships' Boats: A Treatise on the Dangers of the Present System and their Remedy*, Wilson, London, 1859.

27 *The Times*, May 21 1855.

28 *The Supply of Life-boats to the Navy and the Best Mode of Lowering Boats and Saving Life at Sea.* British Sessional Papers, House of Commons, E.L. Erickson (ed), XIV.383, 1872.

29 A. Vizetelly, *Boat Lowering and Disengaging Apparatus*, The Annual Report of the Royal School of Naval Architecture and Marine Engineering, William Denny and Bros., Henry Sotheran and Co., London, 1875.

CHAPTER 4

1 Results of experiments conducted at the Portsmouth Dockyard and reported in *The Times*, 11 February 1861.

2 For official purposes a 'statute adult' was any person over the age of 12 years, with two children aged between 12 months and 12 years also reckoned as equivalent to one 'statute adult.'

3 See comments in *The Times*, 26 December 1874.

4 *East and West London*, Rev. H. Jones, Smith, Elder & Co., 1875.

5 *Ibid.*

6 *The Times*, 12 August 1874.

7 *The East End News*, 29 May 1874.

8 Thomas Love Peacock, A Whitebait Dinner at Lovegroves of Blackwall, July 1851, in: The Halliford Edition of the Works of Thomas Love Peacock, H.F.B. Brett-Smith and C.E. Jones (eds.), Constable and Co., London, 1931.

9 *The PLA Monthly*, October 1930.

10 Emigrants were despatched from the depot at the rate of 2000 a month in mid-1874; a total of 40,000 people immigrated to New Zealand during the year.

11 See 4 above

12 *The East End News*, 29 May 1874.

13 *Otago Daily Times*, 17 January 1874.

14 According to the charter party signed on 7 August 1874 the New Zealand Government agreed to pay Shaw, Savill & Co. £14 10s 0d for every statute adult taken out on the

Cospatrick (see 2 above). Children younger than 12 months of age were carried without charge.

15 An opinion expressed in a *New Zealand Herald* editorial, 23 July 1874.

16 *The Lancet*, 23 May 1874.

17 Testimony of Henry J. Matthew, published in *The Times*, 31 December 1874.

18 Originally British owned, *Sea King* was purchased by the Government of the Confederate States in 1863 and fitted out as a commerce raider. The vessel achieved world-wide notoriety when, renamed *Shenandoah* and under the command of Captain James Waddell, she continued to sink Union shipping long after the American Civil War had ended on 9 April 1865. Fearing that he and his men would be hung as pirates if they entered American waters, Waddell elected to sail the *Shenandoah* to Liverpool, where he surrendered to the British Government on 5 November. The name change was reversed when the vessel was restored to British ownership.

19 *Farringdon Advertiser*, 9 January 1875.

20 *Montrose Standard and Angus and Mearns Register*, 8 January 1875.

21 *Farringdon Advertiser*, 2 January 1875.

22 Regulations to be Observed on Emigrant Ships of the Government of New Zealand, September, 1874, File MT9/99, National Archive, Kew, London.

23 *Ibid.*

24 This diet was very occasionally supplemented by fresh produce: sheep and chickens were carried in pens on the upper deck.

25 Sustained good conduct was something of a rarity on New Zealand-bound emigrant vessels. More typical was the behaviour recorded by emigrant Thomas Payne Judkins, of the sailing ship *Assaye*. On 13 November 1874, when the *Assaye* was 64 days into a voyage to Auckland, Judkins wrote in his journal: 'Upon my word, I can forbear no longer to note the cases of imposition, encroachment and roguery, that have come to my notice on this ship … Many cases of pilfering amongst the emigrants themselves might be recorded, but the writing of such pettifogging cases of dishonesty would, I think, be sufficiently numerous and childish to make one sea-sick. Yes, and here is another pretty go – the third mate in irons. What for? Why, this morning when he came to serve out the provisions he was drunk.' Other journal entries document deaths among the women and children, miscarried pregnancies, a food riot, broaching cargo, and drunkenness among the ship's constables.

26 There was a good reason to be wary of passengers with matches in their possession; in 1848 an emigrant on the ship *Ocean Monarch* lit a fire in a wooden ventilator after mistaking it for a chimney. Three hours later the vessel had burned to the water's edge almost within sight of Liverpool, and 178 of the 396 people on board were dead.

27 To be 'spoken' was to participate in a haphazard system of keeping track of vessels at sea before the advent of marine radio. Chance meetings were reported when each ship next made port. The key information to be handed on was the identity of the other vessel, where from and where bound, and the date and position of the encounter.

28 *The Times*, 5 January 1875.

29 *Otago Police Gazette*, April, 1874. See also *The Otago Daily Times*, 21 March 1874.

30 *The Times*, 4 January 1875.

31 *The Times*, 1 January 1875.

32 *Lloyd's Weekly News*, 3 December 1911.

33 W. Wood, *Survivors' Tales of Famous Shipwrecks*, Bles, London, 1932.

CHAPTER 5

1 The leather-bound original appears not to have survived. Various versions of the text were reported in the press, but this extract, taken from *The Times*, 2 January 1875, is likely to be accurate.

2 Oceanographic data from: *Scientific Results of the German Atlantic Expedition of the Research Vessel Meteor*, 1925-1927. G. Böhnecke, Vol.5.

3 F. Golden and M. Tipton, *Essentials of Sea Survival*, Human Kinetics, 2002.

4 *Montrose, Arbroath and Brechin Review*, 8 January 1875.

5 Romaine's craft also relied on women's clothing for its rig, utilising a shawl for a sail.

6 *The Daily News*, 2 January 1875.

7 The clinical symptoms associated with acute dehydration are described in 3 above.

8 *Challenger* was returning to London from Nelson, New Zealand when she was abandoned in the Atlantic in a sinking condition on 14 May 1871; the American vessel *Twilight* picked up all 31 members of her crew.

9 See *The Times*, 2 January 1875.

10 See *The Times*, 4 January 1875.

11 A fact that he later attributed to his body having absorbed moisture through the skin, while 'constantly saturated' by the breaking seas. Modern research also indicates that keeping the skin wetted is beneficial, see 3 above.

12 See 10 above.

13 In an account by Cotter published in 1911 (see 14 below), the dissector is described as a French Canadian; however, no one matching this description is known to have been on the *Cospatrick*.

14 *Lloyd's Weekly News*, 3 December 1911.

15 The survivors were reluctant to identify the people on whose bodies they had subsisted, but in 1911 Cotter stated that McBride and Freddy Bentley were in the boat just before end, see 14 above. The names of the known occupants of the starboard and port lifeboats are given in Appendix 1.

CHAPTER 6

1 *The Daily News*, 2 January 1875.

2 *Montrose Standard and Angus and Mearns Register*, 5 February 1875.

3 W. Wood, *Survivors' Tales of Famous Shipwrecks*, Bles, London, 1932

4 *The Daily News*, 1 January 1875.

5 *Ibid*.

6 *The Times*, 5 January 1875.

7 Directed to the Earl of Caernarvon, Secretary of State for the Colonies, Janisch's report fully described the circumstances of the disaster in 10 succinct paragraphs. He particularly made the point that 'the ship was very inadequately furnished with boats for so large a number of passengers', and that this insufficiency must 'have rendered a large loss of life inevitable'. The report also condemned 'the impropriety of loading large crowded passenger ships with quantities of inflammable matter, in addition to the living freight', but these censures were not acted upon; see also 6 above.

8 Lloyd's published the contents of the Madeira telegram on Monday, 28 December, but did not indicate the likely number of lives lost.

9 The confusion arose because *Cospatrick*'s longitude at the time of her destruction was mistakenly given as 12° W, rather than 12° E.

10 These figures relate to place of birth rather than residence. The emigrants also included seven French and one Swiss.

11 From the *North British Daily Mail*, see 1 above.

12 The contents of the telegram were published in *The Times* on Thursday, 31 December 1874.

13 The payments were reputed to be £100 to McDonald and £25 each to Cotter and Lewis. Cotter later claimed that McDonald received £60 from Forbes, which he refused to share.

14 *The Daily News*, 1 January 1875.

15 *The Daily Chronicle*, 2 January 1875; see also 14 above.

16 *The Daily News*, 2 January 1875.

17 *The Penny Illustrated Paper* of 9 January 1875 proffered the opinion that the occasion had reduced the English press to 'the level of some of those American journals which hold no sorrow sacred, no privacy inviolable, no circumstance too painful, no catastrophe too harrowing, no individual convictions too solemn and awful for the hard and repulsive intrusion of interviewers.'

18 *The Cornish Telegraph*, 6 January 1875.

19 *The Weekly Express* (Jersey), 9 January 1875.

20 Actions that included murder; see editorial comments in 18 above, for example: 'What they admit they did is bad enough; what they really did was worse – and it will never fully be known. It's a sickening story.' It was also reported (see 15 above) that Lewis spoke of three women in McDonald's boat, who 'had to be held, or they would have jumped in the sea, and when, one by one they died, they were eaten.' The story appears to be invention, however.

21 *Montrose, Arbroath and Brechin Review*, 8 January 1875.

22 Collections to assist the victims of shipwreck were not always popular; no sooner had the fund been established than it attracted criticism in *The Times* of 1 January 1875, with one correspondent writing in the belief that *Cospatrick*'s agricultural poor were unworthy, and their dependents more so: 'Attention (should be drawn) to the facts to prevent people squandering, in a fit of sensational enthusiasm, money which might be more rationally and usefully employed.' Such views did not stop the fund from accumulating to a total of just under £3500. On 9 March 1875 the Mansion House disbursed the sum of £2700, granting £500 to Jean and Jessie Elmslie, and £865 to the near and dependent relatives of those of the crew who were lost. An additional sum of £542 was distributed among various claimants later in the year and the fund was closed. There is no record of the amounts paid to the three survivors.

23 McDonald's comments regarding Nicholas Birbeck's presence in the boat are reported in *The Scotsman* of 11 January 1875. The same article reports the fate of Birbeck's 23-year-old brother, John – drowned during the attempted launching of the boat.

24 The depositions of the survivors were widely published; see, for example, *The Times* of 5 January 1875.

25 Only verbal descriptions of the layout of *Cospatrick*'s forward section were given to the various inquiries held in 1875. It appears that the vessel's building plan no longer exists.

26 Desposition of Thomas Lewis, see 24 above.

27 It was also believed that the coal would smoulder for days before igniting – a process which would have been betrayed by the resulting smoke and smell.

28 *The Times*, 5 January 1875.

29 *Ibid*.

30 McDonald later spoke in 'strong terms' against this conduct; see the *Montrose Standard and Angus and Mearns Register*, 8 January 1875.

31 This was evident from statements made in 1885; see the Dundee Royal Lunatic Asylum casebook for Charles Henry McDonald, patient #3836, 1884–5, Dundee University Archive.

CHAPTER 7

1 *The Times*, 9 February 1875.
2 *The Times*, 1 January 1875.
3 See, for example, letters to the editor of *The Times* published on 4, 5, 6, 8, 11, 12 and 13 January.
4 There were no casualties even though 368 troops and a number of dependants were being carried. This latter group, comprising '8 women, 7 children and a number of ladies, relatives of the officers', was placed in a well-provisioned boat, which lay off at a distance while the fire was fought. It was fortunate that the craft was fitted with Clifford's 'Patent Boat Lowering Gear', for it was 'lowered by [this device] without the slightest accident although there was a heavy sea running at the time.' Castle would not have risked launching the boat had it been equipped with conventional falls (see *The Times* of 29 December 1857 and a personal communication from Captain John Castle to Charles Clifford reported in *The Times*, 4 March 1859).
5 *Report of the Court of Inquiry.* British Seasonal Papers, House of Commons, E.L. Erickson (ed.), LXX.33, 1875.
6 File MT 9/99, M 535, 1875. National Archive, Kew, London. Forster's reply is contained in the same file.
7 Emigration officers were guided by rules laid down in the 1855 Passengers Act. They could object to the presence of gunpowder, corrosive acids or articles liable to spontaneous combustion, but much had changed since the Act first came into force. Explosives such as dynamite and many petroleum-based solvents and oils that were unknown in 1855 were in widespread use by 1874. In the absence of specific instructions designating flammable items as dangerous, officers usually concurred when these were stowed alongside general merchandise.
8 Suggestion made to Isaac Carter, of the stevedoring firm Westhorp & Co., by Arthur Cohen, QC, counsel for the Board of Trade. See *The Times*, 5 February 1875.
9 *The Times*, 6 February 1875.
10 See 5 above.
11 *The Times* 6 January 1875.
12 *Ibid.*
13 W. Wood, *Survivors' Tales of Famous Shipwrecks*, Bles, London, 1932.
14 The opinion of Captain William Braddick of the *Countess of Kintore* and contained in a letter written by him on 7 February 1875. Braddick had served on the *Cospatrick* as second mate under Elmslie in 1868. Excerpts from the letter appear in the *Otago Witness*, 3 April 1875.
15 See 9 above.
16 See 5 above.
17 *The Times*, 9 January and 8 March 1875.
18 *Otago Daily Times*, 10 March 1875.
19 *Broaching Cargo at Sea: Loss of the Cospatrick*, (correspondence relating to). Letter to the Right Hon. Earl of Carnarvon from the Hon. J. Vogel (3 May 1875). House of the General Assembly of New Zealand, No. 1, H.1, 1876.
20 *The Times*, 2 October 1875.
21 Excerpts from the letter were published in *The Times*, 23 October 1875.
22 *The Times*, 25 December 1876.

23 News of the loss was transmitted from Britain to Melbourne by electric telegraph, and carried to New Zealand by the steamer *Omeo*. This vessel reached the southern port of Bluff on 10 January and the news was then telegraphed to Auckland. *Cospatrick*'s loss was also deeply felt in Melbourne, where the vessel was well known as a consequence of her 1871 visit.

24 The *Evening Star* (Auckland), 11 January 1875.

25 Featherston V. Savill, Queens Bench Division, High Court of Justice, 1 Febuary 1876. See IM 5/H/12+13, No.126, National Archives, Wellington, New Zealand

26 H. Brett, *White Wings, Fifty Years of Sail in the New Zealand Trade, 1850 to 1900* Vol 1., Brett Printing, Auckland, 1924.

27 *The Times*, 26 May 1873.

28 K. Tiller (ed.), *Wychwood History, Milton and Shipton in the Nineteenth Century*, Chap. IV. Wychwood Local History Society and Oxford University Department for External Studies, 1987.

29 *Tables Showing the Progress of British Merchant Shipping*. British Sessional Papers, House of Commons, E.L. Erickson (ed.), LXVI.1, 1876; LXXVII.1, 1900.

30 *Appendix P to the Report from the Select Committee for Saving Life at Sea*. British Sessional Papers, House of Commons, E.L. Erickson (ed.), XII.1, 1887.

31 Some shipping companies added boat capacity considerably in excess of the legal minimum. In 1887 Cunard, White Star's main transatlantic rival and a company with an almost unblemished safety record stretching back over 50 years, provided double the boat accommodation of her competitor. See: *Report by the Board of Trade on Questions of Boats, Rafts and Life-saving Appliances*. British Sessional Papers, House of Commons, E.L. Erickson (ed.), LXXIII.457, 1887.

32 As a 'colonial registered' British vessel, the safety regulations applying to the *Sir John Lawrence* differed somewhat from those applying to UK registered vessels.

33 The *Sir John Lawrence* carried four boats, two of which were 'lifeboats'.

34 *Proceedings of a Marine Court of Inquiry held at the Post Office, Calcutta*, 11 July 1887; File MT9/317, Public Record Office, Kew, London.

35 *Ibid*.

36 *Report from the Select Committee on Saving Life at sea*. British Sessional papers, House of Commons, E.L. Erickson (ed.) XII.1, 1887.

37 Gray, who died in 1890 aged 58, was the author of a 72-page booklet (*Under the Red Ensign, or Going to Sea*, Simpkin Marshall & Co., London, 1878), which gave useful information to boys contemplating a career at sea … 'In all cases, a strong heavy lad who can pull his weight in beef at the end of a rope is of more value than another.'

38 Thomas Gray, *Observations on the Rules of the Road at Sea*, J.D. Potter, London, 1878.

39 *Nautical Magazine*, 1885.

40 See *The Times*, 7 August 1885; the newspaper published several letters on the subject later in the month.

41 See 39 above.

42 However, this idea appears to have originated with the Dumbarton shipbuilder William Denny, who suggested a 'Board of Control' of similar composition before the 1885 Royal Commission on Loss of Life at Sea.

43 *Report made to the Board of Trade by the Committee Appointed by that Board in Pursuance of the Merchant Shipping (Life Saving Appliances) Act*. British Sessional Papers, House of Commons, E.L. Erickson (ed.), LXIX.171, 1889.

44 Figures taken from the United States Senate Inquiry.

45 Statement by J. Bruce Ismay, President of the White Star Line, published in *The Times*, 22 April 1912.

46 As well as the USA and Great Britain, signatories to the convention were Canada, Australia, New Zealand, Germany, France, Austria-Hungary, Italy, Spain, Sweden, Norway, Belgium, and Denmark; however, owing to the intervention of the First World War the convention was not fully implemented until 1927.

47 *Law Journal Reports*, Statutes, Vol. LXXXIII, 1914.

CHAPTER 8

1 They were Kate and William Harvey, Mary and Edward Whitehead and their 11-day-old infant, Caroline and John Marsh, and Catherine and Bartholomew Geary.

2 R. Williams, *The Survival of Twm Pen-Stryd, a Moelfre Seaman*, Cymgen, Portaethwy, 1974.

3 Only 41 survivors, all male, were rescued from a ship's complement of 487. See the table on page 31 of this volume, and *The Golden Wreck. The Tragedy of the Royal Charter*, A. McKee, Souvenir, London, 1986.

4 Letter to *The Times*, Lord Shaftesbury and W. Williams, 29 March 1866.

5 *Chichester* Record of Edward Cotter, #190, Shaftesbury Homes and Arethusa, 1872–3.

6 *Chichester* Record of William James Wood, #122, Shaftesbury Homes and Arethusa, 1874.

7 J. Thurburn, *Chichester* Training Ship, Report to the Committee, Shaftesbury Homes and Arethusa, 1872.

8 See 5 above.

9 W. Gilbert, *Chichester* Training Ship, *The Evening News*, p. 477, 1874.

10 *Otago Police Gazette*, April, 1874; see also the *Otago Daily Times*, 21 March 1874.

11 W. Wood, *Survivors' Tales of Famous Shipwrecks*, Bles, London, 1932.

12 Records of the Metropolitan Fire Brigade (London) for Edward Cotter #1,222, 1878.

13 Records of the Metropolitan Fire Brigade (London) for Edward Cotter #2,802, 1891–3.

14 See 5 above; the year of his birth is verified by the census of 1871, (taken in April), which reports him as 13 years of age and London born (although of Irish parentage). Cotter subtracted six years from his true age at the time of his re-enlistment in the Metropolitan Fire Brigade (see 13 above) and marriage and death certificates confirm that he maintained the fiction throughout the remainder of his life.

15 See 13 above.

16 *Lloyd's Weekly News*, 3 December 1911.

17 See 11 above.

18 S. Waters, *Shaw Savill, 100 years of Trading*, Whitcombe and Tombes, Christchurch, 1961.

19 However, a young Timaru waterman named Henry McDonald did lose his life in the *Ben Venue* incident.

20 H. Brett, *White Wings, Fifty Years of Sail in the New Zealand Trade, 1850 to 1900*, Vol. 1, Brett Printing, Auckland, 1924.

21 *Montrose Standard and Angus and Mearns Register*, 5 February 1875.

22 *The Daily News*, 1 January 1875.

23 Dundee Royal Lunatic Asylum casebook for Charles Henry McDonald, patient #3836, 1884–5, Dundee University Archive.

SOURCES OF ILLUSTRATIONS

Author: pp. 55, 113, 123; Bancroft and Local History Library: p. 57; British Library Newspaper Library: front cover and pp. 24, 26, 29, 41, 43, 51 (bottom), 60, 69, 70, 89; David Savill: back cover* and p. 21; Dunedin Public Library: p. 111; Ian J. Farquhar: p. 19; Montrose Public Library: p. 53; National Archives, London: p. 99; National Maritime Museum, Greenwich: pp. 48, 51 (top), 91; Otago Settlers' Museum: pp. 23, 76; Shaftesbury Homes and Arethusa: pp. 63, 93, 120, 125, 127; University of Otago Library: p. 61.

*Reproduced from *Sail to New Zealand* by David Savill; however, we have been unable to determine whether copyright is held on this item.

INDEX

Numbers in bold indicate illustrations.

Ada Melmore: 30
Adderley, Sir Charles: 103
Adriatic: 115
Albuera: 60
Amberwitch: 20, 140
America: 35, 36
Anazi: 61
Anderson, John: 91, 156
Archer, James: 12–16
Arracan: 10, 11
Assaye: 20, 140
Atlantic: 28, 29, 31, 45–47
Atwell, Hubert: 62, 148
Avalanche: 61

Ben Venue: 129
Bentley, Thomas: 78, 79, 82, 85, 97,
    131, 150
Bentley, Frederick: 79, 85, 97, 131, 150,
    165
Berthon, Rev. E.L.: 38
Bickersteth, Edward: 82, 97, 131, 150
Biddiss, Thomas: 42, 44
Birbeck, Nicholas: 97, 156, 166
Birkenhead: 30–33
Blervie Castle: 18
Board of Trade: 15, 35, 37, 38, 40, 41,
    43, 50, 102–105, 107, 110, 115–118
Boynton, Paul: 104
Brady, Cornelius: 46, 47
British Sceptre: 87, 88, 90, 112, 129
Brunswick Hotel: 56–58
Bunt, John: 128, 131
    and wife Sarah, 97, 151
Byron, Robert: 78, 131, 151

Cadle, James F.: 59, 60, 63–65, 67, 72,
    75, 148
Cannibalism: 10, 15, 16, 39
Cargo plundering: 109–111
Castle, John: 104–106, 166
Cathcart: 110
Challenger: 82, 165
Chichester: 124, 125, **125**, 126, 128

City of Glasgow: 28
City of Manchester: 11
Clifford, Charles: 50
    and 'Patent Boat Lowering Gear',
    49–52, **51**, 55, 64, 74, 167
Coal, spontaneous combustion of: 10, 98
Cohen, Arthur: 105–107, 167
Collapsible boats: 38
Cope, Peter: 80, 96, 131, 148
Cospatrick: 16, **23**, 28, 31, 52, 53, 59–65.
    63, 83, 111–114, 118
    Advertisement for sale of photograph
    of, **111**
    and cannibalism, 10, 83, 92, 94, 95,
    126, 165, 166
    as a cable–layer, 19, 20, 140
    Board of Trade inquiry into loss, 102,
    104–109, 128
    Boats, 54, 55, **76**, 77, 90, 108, 112,
    121, 122, 165
    Burning of, 10, 29, 66–76, **69**, **70**
    Cargo, 53, 96, 100
    Description of, 17
    Final sailing notice of, **61**
    Fitting out, 54
    Lifeboat occupants, 77–86, 96, 97,
    121, 131, **89**
    Passenger births and deaths on, 17,
    23, 145–147
    Memorial, **113**
    Receiver of Wreck inquiry into loss:
    97, 98
    Relief fund: 166
    Sinking of: 80
    Voyages of, 17–25, 138–143
Cossipore: 82
Cotter, Edward: 72–74, 77, 79, 83–85, 88,
    90, 92, **93**, 94–98, 105, 108, **120**,
    122, 124–129, **127**, 131, 165, 166,
    169
Crompton, Henry: 66, 67, 73

Dallam Tower: 125, 126
Davits, radial (see also Lifeboats and Ships'
    boats): **49**
Dover Castle: 113

Dunbar: 18
Dunbar, Duncan: 17–19, **19**
Duncan Dunbar: 18
Dunfillan: 59
Dutton, Alfred: 77, 131, 148
Easter, John: 41, 44
Edwin Fox: 22
Ellis, Henry: 15, 16
Elmslie, Alexander: 17, 22, 24, 62, 64, 66,
    67, 71, 74, 108, 141–143
    and wife Henrietta, 60, **60**, 75
    Children of, 60, 166
Elmslie, James Aberdour: 17, 60, 61,
    139–141
Emigrant ships (see also Passenger ships):
    28–30, 33, 52, 56, 59, 60, 104, 110
Emigration: 22, 33, 109, 110, 114
    Advertisement to encourage, **53**
Euxine: 39, 161
    Burning of, 12,
    Survivors from, 12–16

Farrer, T.H.: 105
Fearon, Stephen: 23
Featherstone, Isaac: 56, 98, 102, 110, 111
Fire-pumps: 10,
    Downton, 54, **55**, 67
Fitzgerald, Robert: 63, 65
    and wife Mary, 72, 152
Forbes, Archibald: 92, 94, 95, 130
Forster, John (Capt.): 61, 105
Fraser, William T.: 15
Firth, J.W.: 36

Gadsun, Rev. J.: 61, 62
Gioffus, Francis: 12–15
Glenlora: 61, 112
Godliaton, Robert: 64, 148

Golden Fleece: 24
Gray, Thomas: 16, 116, 117, 168

Hamilton, Robert: 80, 83, 86, 88, 122,
    131, 148
Hancock, Charles: 72, 77, 131, 148
Harvey, Catherine: 78, 79, 131, 159
Heath Park: 24, 161
Hedges, Richard: 114, 152
Hindley (Linley), John: 46

Hodge, G.: 17, 138
Hudson, 61, 126

Jackson, Peter: 12, 13
Jahnke, William: 87–90, 112, 129
Janisch, Hudson: 90
    Report on Cospatrick disaster by, 165
Java Packet: 15
Jones, Brasher: 73, 148
Jones, Bridget: 67, 153

Kapunda: 28–31
King, William: 80, 148
Kynaston, A.F. (Lieut.): 49
Kynaston, C.M. (Capt.), and boat-
    disengaging mechanism: 50, 52
Knowles, Edward: 39–42
Knowles, Fredericka: 40–42

Lady Jocelyn: 61, 128
Langstone: 25, 61
Leech, John: 116
Leuchan, Jeremiah: 85, 86, 88, 97, 131,
    157
Lewis, Thomas (Quartermaster): 65, 66,
    77, 79, 83–86, 88, 90, 92, **93**, 94, 95,
    98, 105, **120**, 122–124, 131, 166
Lifeboats (see also Ships' Boats): 37,
    47–52, 115–119
Livingstone, Robert, John and William:
    91, 157
Llanallgo churchyard, Moelfre: 123, **123**,
    124
Lutterworth: 110, 111

Marlborough: 61
McBride, John: 85, 97, 131, 158, 165
McDonald, Henry: 16, 24, **24**, 25, 62, 64,
    65, 72–74, 77, 79–90, 92, 93, 94–98,
    100–102, 105, 108, **120**, 121, 122,
    128–131, 161, 166
    and brother Osmond, 102, 161
    and wife Jane, 62, 102, 129, 130
    Letter to Shaw Savill from, **99**
McNeill, John (Scottie): 78, 80, 82, 131,
    148
McQueen: Maggie: 91, 159
Merchant Shipping Act: 110
    of 1854, 35

of 1875, 44
of 1894, 117
Metcalfe, H.J.: 47
Metropolitan Fire Brigade: 126–128, 169
Müller, August, 12–16
Murdoch, Peter, 12, 161
Murray, Sir Digby: 115, 116
Murrillo, 42, 43
Napier, William (Lieut. Gen.): 32
Neustein, William: 116
New Mains: 91, 92
New Zealand Emigration Depot: 55–59, **57**, 162
New Zealand Shipping Company: 21, 59
Northfleet: 18, 28, 31, 39–45, 118
'The Captain's Farewell', **43**
'The Rush for the Boats', **41**
Nyanza: 90, **91**, 92, 94

Ocean Monarch: 164
Owens, Edward: 46, 47

Paddle-box boats: 31, 32
Passenger ships (see also Emigrant ships): 31, 35–39, 45, 50, 108, 109, 111, 115–119
Passengers Act of 1855: 37, 167
Clause 27 of, 35, 39, 115
Patteson, James: 104, 105, 107, 108
Perseverance: 38, 39
Persian Gulf Telegraph Cable: 19, 20, 140
Pillow, Thomas: 101, 148
Plimsoll, Samuel: 44, 49, 103
Pryce, Charles: 104, 106

Queen of the Age: 110

Reynolds, George: 12, 13
Romaine, Charles: 25, 65, 67, 73–76, 79–82, 90, 91, 121, 131, 148, 165
Royal Charter: 28, 31, 124

Salmond, Robert: 30, 32, 33
Sandström, Victor: 12–16
Sarah Sands: 105
Sartorious, George (Admiral): 104
Savill, Walter: 20, 21, **21**, 22

Schutt, Manus: 12–14, 16
Scott, Charles: 17, 138–139
Sea King: 61, 164
Seamen: 122
Mortality among, 27, 44
Perception of: 39
Seaton (Maj.): 32
Shaftesbury, Lord: 124
Shaw, Robert: 21
Shaw, Savill & Co. (Shaw Savill): 20, 59, 60, 61, 90, 94–96, 102–104, 107, 110, 112, 129, 163
Shea, Mary: 74, 80, 131
Shenandoah: 164
Ships' boats (see also Lifeboats): **48**, **51**
Occupancy of, 38, 161
Requirements: 38
Stowage of, 36
Types, 37, 38, 48
Shipton-under-Wychwood: 91, 113, 114
Shipwrecks, nineteenth century:
Frequency of, 9, **26**, 27, 56
Major incidents, 28–30
Survival statistics, table of, 31
Sir John Lawrence: 28, 115, 116, 168
Smith, Edward: 54, 55, 98, 100–102, 106, 107
Smith, G. (Capt.): 31
SOLAS: 119
Speakman, John: 46, 47
St Leonards: 129
Stockton, J.C.: 97, 98
Strathmore: 110, 111
Surat: 56
Symons, William: 73, 101, 129, 148

Tayleur: 28, 29, 31, 33–35
Temple, James: 20, 96, 103, 104, 107
Thomas, Robert: 46, 47
Thurburn, James: 125
Tintern Abbey: 107
Titanic: 38, 117, 118
Torrance, John: 91, 158
Townsend, Henry: 114, 155
Turner, William: 104
Tweed: 110, 140

Utopia: 28–31, **29**

Vermeulen, Alexander: 12, 13, 16
Vogel, Julius: 109, 110

Wakefield, Thomas: 72, 148
Walpole, Walter: 24
Ward, J.R. (Capt.): 47, 48
Webster, David: 10, 12, 16
    Award of George Medal to, 11
Whitehead, Mary and Edward: 65, 74,
    131, 156

William Brown: 161, 162
Williams, Charles: 126, 132
Williams, J.A.: 45, 47
Wilson, Archibald: 38, 39
Wood, William: 74, 77, 124, 125, 131,
    148
Wray, Mary and William: 75, 156
Wright, E.C.W. (Capt.): 32